The Audacity of
Survival

The Audacity of
Survival

AN OPULENT EXPERIENCE

DHUSHIYANTHA KULADEVA

PARTRIDGE

A Penguin Random House Company

To order additional copies of this book, contact
Toll Free 800 101 2657 (Singapore)
Toll Free 1 800 81 7340 (Malaysia)
orders.singapore@partridgepublishing.com

www.partridgepublishing.com/singapore

Contents

SYNOPSIS

The Audacity of Survival – An opulent experience - is a personal account that obscures an extraordinary journey and a relentless story of life worth living. Dhush Kuladeva, as he is known within his inner circle, was raised by parents who were both teachers, and he was fortunate and blessed to have been surrounded by a large extended family, whose insatiable thirst for knowledge and a solid education platform was second to none. Dhush grew up in a small town in Malaysia, and gained his early education in Muar, Johor and subsequently in St. Paul's Institution, Seremban. After leaving school, he went on to complete his South Australian Matriculation at Taylor's College Kuala Lumpur, and as fate would have it, was admitted to an Institute of Advanced Education at Warrnambool, Victoria, Australia (later known as Deakin Warrnambool).

His initial area of study was in the school of business majoring in Accounting, but he soon found this to be too rigid and limited. Switching to The Social Sciences was the best decision he ever made, as it resulted in his ability to polish up his interpersonal skills and relationships that he had fostered during his university days, and this rewarded him with a Degree in The Social Sciences, majoring in Psychology and Sociology. The Australian education system worked well with his personal "blue print", and it enabled him to grow exponentially, while shaping the path to self-discovery. Dhush was always fascinated with the human spirit and what makes us all "tick"! His love for the human experience enabled him to further embark on individual research into various areas of human behaviour, clinical psychology, philosophy and sociology.

After graduation, Dhush embarked on a rather bold move by gaining employment in an independent family owned and operated establishment, with a special emphasis on Hand Knotted Oriental Carpets and Rugs. He had a burning desire to know more about the "art form" and the ingenious weavers who applied their sheer talent into creating such amazing works of expression. Each had a story to tell, and this basically stamped his love for the splendour of The Orient, from the Tents, Cottages and Workshops of Central Asia. From then on, Dhush never looked back, and in his quest to prevail, despite the challenging odds that he faced later on in his life, saw an ensemble of creativity, that centred around reinventing and defining an unprecedented journey of a self-fulfilling prophecy. He applied symmetrical and asymmetrical approaches towards solving the most intense of issues and situations, and in his personal mission and discourse, came to a realization that everything that appeared to be in a state of calamity actually made sense. There was some "method in the madness" that seemed to resonate within his inner psyche, and his fundamental justification of survival centred on the fact that the human condition was a result of our seemingly apparent state of "registering" – all the time, and even in a dream-like state. The spirit of the human condition was so powerful, that we have the ability to grow exponentially, even if it meant that it had to be within the parameters of illness or disease. Living life against all odds was never tantamount to a death sentence, especially when one has been diagnosed with cancer, advanced cancer, at that. Dhush simplified his approach, and made a promise that each day needed to be approached with dignity and strength, and that each day, even if it meant living with limited time, needed to be experienced with extraordinary audacity.

In this attempt to put everything into perspective in his very first book, he couldn't help but feel sorry for himself at times, but soon realized that he needed to break away from the clutches of self-imposed misery. Pain was a part of life, but suffering was a choice, and he wasn't about to make that choice. He despised failure, and loved the attention he would get from people who seemed to gravitate towards him. A dear friend said that he had the ability to make a difference while sharing his leaflets of self-determination. This meant that whatever negative aspects surrounding his life could be made to disappear through the transformation of an idea or a transformation into an idea, even if it meant that life's daily doses needed to be purchased in small doses, twenty four hours at a time.

In The Audacity of Survival, Dhush talks about his opulent experience while living with Cancer for almost twenty years, and took to the sheer brilliance of palette and fleece in the fascinating area of carpets as a means of healing. Intensity of colours, its kaleidoscope of motifs and intentions, together with its relationship within all spatial elements, created a sense of continuity and longevity in acceptable doses. The element of sophistication was replaced with profundity at its core element. Dhush was able to simply get things done by breaking down the walls that he had initially erected around him, and soon began to realize and reaffirm his belief, that life needed to be lived according to sheer will and a certain level of determinism, and it wasn't about following a set of rules within which, life could very well be perceived as a series of trials and tribulations that would end up wasting precious time. This resulted in his ability to deal with his illness, and move on with his personal quest and throughout the journey to this very day,

Dhush credits his presence and existence on earth to the people around him especially his family, his dearly departed father, whose values and choices shaped the man he is today, his mother, whose tenacity and spirited approach to life enabled him to reinvent his relationship with her. Having lost his father at the age of twenty, Dhush forged a new bond with his mother, a powerful portrait of a woman, who inevitably had to regain her independence over a period of time, and continues to play a very significant part in his life. Not forgetting his brother and sister, both of whom had an incredible influence on his life from his early upbringing, and the raw honesty that they have shared collectively, enabled him to foster a relationship with them which has been tried and tested on a solid foundation of character building. In his quest to discover his journey right to this very day, Dhush continues to be sensitive towards relationships fostered over time, and lives in an existential infrastructure that makes sense to him.

Dhush Kuladeva is married to his long-time companion Rozana, and has a home in Singapore and shuttles between his family home and his love for his work in Vietnam. This journey begins with his sincere appreciation for his wife, who gave him the opportunity to discover himself unconditionally.

The Audacity of Survival:
An Opulent Experience

"I seek to build a platform of meditations on tradition by imagining, intuiting and reinventing. To understand unique and subtle variations in my life is the abyss in spatial dimensions, taking symmetrical and asymmetrical approaches to solving the most intense of issues and situations. Intermittently, and "abrash" in intensity would occur – dialogues and decisions altered, and everything around me that seemed imperfect would make perfect sense".

Dhush Kuladeva

INTRODUCTION

RAJIV KULADEVA

"To go to the limit is not only to resist but also to let oneself go. I need to sense myself as the sense of what exceeds me. I sometimes need to write things which in part escape me, but which are an exact proof of that which, in me, is beyond me."

Dhushiyantha Kuladeva, my only brother, has written a book about the "teaching" of *An Opulent Experience*. In relation to the material thinking it enjoins, it displays the possibility of Ana-materialistic thinking, the recovery from the materials of thinking certain immanent issues in life or tendencies towards higher levels of self-organisation. These "assemblages" are simultaneously associations of ideas and the "existential infrastructure for life." They are disposed to join together in new ways that are conducive to producing the conditions where life is lived twice, constructively and re-constructively, actively and reflectively. His Ana-materialism can be characterised as a marriage of phenomenological principles of analysis to the inherent indeterminism of complex systems whose behaviour is—like the approach he recommends to life—non-linear, that is, both scripturally and ethically, open, unfinished, receptive to innovation. The grounds for bringing out the immanence of life do not reside outside the field of reflection - in some kind of etymological Urspraches. They lie—and this is the poetic brio as well as ethical concern of his pedagogy—in the pathways discovered between different semantic and phonological nuances: perfecting the process of path finding is the aspiration of his propaedeutic.

With the example of Heidegger in mind, Kuladeva gathers rather than collects; more radically, because of his commitment to holding different meanings together, he does not lay concepts side by side but subjects them to a prior scrutiny to determine their fitness for being joined together—to gather implies what Kuladeva takes to be the fundamental justification of Survival, the fact that human being is "being-in-common" and it is the birth of life itself—the bringing out of the potential jointure of things— that permits this to be.

At the heart of this meditation is Kuladeva's concern to recuperate the Western clearing of thought for a new, more sustainable ecology of living with and alongside. His pathways into the thick of things look for what is suitable or well-fitted to be gathered; the place of gathering is one of adornment, not stripping bare. The art of arrangement reflects a propensity of ideas themselves when their power of self-reorganisation is admitted: in this case there is no violence in bringing the unrelated together. Discovery is the immanence of matter released through its recollection.

Yet the achievement of this book is not to give a new, contemporary vitality and relevance to an ancient trope—the identification of hope with the arches of truth. It is to use an extraordinarily bold and poetic technique of reading thought to show forth life in ideas. In this, etymology does not descend angel-like to inscribe our confusion with order: it originates instead in a prior wonderment at the givenness of the world and its inherent capacity to self-organise.

It is also to be a good physician for, although Kuladeva offers the reader a program for wellbeing, we cannot fail to read what he writes against a background of dis-ease: the urbanism of the megalopolis, the shelter less purlieu of the political, the environmental and the economic refugee and the distress of the soul-warped, provide the background to what is argued, proposed and committed to. A circumambient psychic dishevelment lends his Ana- materialism its urgency. His dream is to recuperate the word (the idea, logos) through a steady showing of its application to the improvement of life. "If misdirected emotions or ideas can be transformed into illness, why not illness could disappear through a transformation into an idea"—attempted is a mode of logophania, the appearance of a coherent "assemblage" of directions for life serving to liberate the collective imagination of its illness.

This is the extraordinary poetic economy of the writing: to house ideas in their rightful places, to build for readers with visions of the world, new patterns of living that are familiar to us because they come as echoes from a primary way of life that is articulate—not defensively self- explanatory but reunited with its logophanic potential, its power to create existential infrastructure, giving shelter less thought a role and voice.

A book of scaffolding, of footholds and handholds, exhibiting a lover's sensitivity to the relationships that make sense of the world, provisional in so many seemly and instructive ways, it is provisional in its generosity.

Rajiv Kuladeva – My brother

SPECIAL CONTRIBUTIONS

BY SHANTI JACQUELINE

I will never forget the day I met you, Dhush Kuladeva.

It was a perfectly normal day in May of 1983 when he decided that the newest kid in College was in need of some friends. And in that trademark incorrigible and tenacious style of his, he just went after what he set his heart and mind on.

I am ever so grateful for your tenacity. Life was never meant to be normal. It was always meant to be extraordinary.

College was the then Taylors' College in Kuala Lumpur. It was probably the only college in the 80s where those of us wanting to pursue tertiary education in Australia or Canada could go to complete our pre-university. Both of us were enrolled in the South Australian Matriculation program; Dhush was a year my senior and had lots of friends; his wit, confidence, that impish smile he has for everyone; he was (and still is) a magnet, to both the guys and the girls, young and old.

But for a fresh from school, small town girl, confident suave Dhush made me nervous and unsure. I don't know if he sensed it but Dhush never let up in trying to be my friend, win my confidence, and make me his friend. He made me comfortable with laughter – his silly, saucy jokes and innuendos made me laugh at every turn. He used to tease me mercilessly too. And yet, we could kickback and talk about our inner most thoughts, fears and dreams without fear of being ridiculed or judged. He made me his friend, and his friends made me theirs as well.

And then there was the party scene. Don't ask me where we found the time or the money to party; we WERE meant to be studying but party we did! Those were the days of the Shakey's Pizza one cent beer every Thursday night. Pay regular price for 1 beer and get your second glass for a mere one cent!! As you can imagine we were in student heaven. How we made it to class the next day is beyond me.

As I write this, I find myself reminiscing, smiling, laughing to myself, feeling fearful and sad, and crying even and finally utterly grateful to the powers that be for blessing us with this thing called friendship. Someone once said *'Friendship is not one big thing; it's a million little things';* and it's these million little things that has allowed a friendship that started out as a chance meeting one normal day in May to last over 30+ years.

Along the years, we've had some great parties with massive hangovers; huge cookouts and yet more hangovers; we've dealt with our fair share of disappointment, heartbreak and bad news, shed tears together, cursed the world together and then, we would be out there again painting the town red earning yet another one of those hangovers. We celebrated each of us finding our life partners, taking the time to get to know both Mike and Rose, and to make room in our lives for them. We were happy because the other was happy. We were troubled because the other was troubled. Families accepted us with open arms, always welcoming, accepting and trusting. We baby - sat pets and homes. We drove each other up the wall when working together on home improvements and probably said never again! ☺ There were some really scary times too where all we could do was pray for each other; pray for strength and comfort and somehow wish that we could trade places. We spend hours discussing recent events, conspiracy theories and even perhaps pretend we know it all. We go silent on each other always confident that we will be able to connect again anytime, anywhere.

These are Mike's and my million little things Dhush.

Thank you for sharing your life with us, always giving, always there and present, always tenacious in everything you do. Thank you for showing the both of us what life and its tribulations are all about. Your journey in life as long as we've known you has had its great moments and some 'tsunamis' too, and seeing you go through it, experiencing all of it with you has been a tremendous humbling yet enriching experience. Looking forward to our next millions of little things!!

Much Love
Shanti & Mike

Shanti Jacqueline, with her husband Michael –
with Dhush and Rajiv Kuladeva

BY MARCIA JAYNE DOWNES

"..Good friends are like stars. You don't always see them, but you know they're always there..."

Looking back over the years (before employment, husband, children and different ways of living life) I have realized, and a lot of this is due to my dear friend Dhushiyantha, that I was privileged to have met an awesome group of people. First year at 'Uni' found lifelong friends; I just didn't realize it then!! Our, unknown to us, establishing group of soulful, slightly crazy, intelligent, slightly untamed friends mixed with routine days and nights of studying and partying was the life we knew. It was a diverse, life changing, analytical, fun and turbulently emotional life we led. And it was, understatedly, the best of times.

I remember Dhush entering into our lives, sharing tutorials, lectures and of course his still famous expression to "Party", gracing us with his refined and charming presence, yet seemingly cautious attributes...then, we got to know him!! To me he seemed (and still is) a true gentleman with high and loving morals. I found that even though I was living away from my family, experiencing the 'parent free', independent new life that 'University was giving me, like Dhush, the loyalty, love and traditions I had grown up with still followed me, and for that, I think we could always relate to each other and pledged the bond we have today.

Following Graduation, I embarked on my first overseas holiday (other than my family's trip and relocation to Australia from England when I was young). I travelled on my own to visit my friend in Singapore and Malaysia (1991). It was the most fabulous of holidays and a most humbling experience. Not only did I stay with Dhush and meet his lovely girlfriend (now wife) Rose, his brother Rajiv and friend James, I learned about and experienced local customs and traditions. I loved it all, and had an incredible load of fun and adventure, not to mention being privy to Dhush's amazing culinary delights.

It felt like we were back in "Kepler St" or "Dhush's Flat" in Warrnambool again. I was treated like a queen. That was the last time I had physical contact with Dhush, as I met my future husband soon after my trip, and maintained to this day a group of beautiful friends that still, like me, chose to keep Warrnambool as their coastal home. It was a completely different existence to that of 'Uni' life with working in the disability area, getting married, to bearing children and experiencing happy adventures and unfortunately sad losses too... our dear friend Allistair (Al) had passed away, which brought a lot of us together again, and for me, my beautiful mother had passed in 1997 (when my first born was only seven months old)..However, in some very tough times, I found solace in knowing my mother, was and is in fact my guiding Angel.

Thanks to modern technology, a few years ago, Dhush and I reconnected through the Facebook network. I remember our very first exciting texted conversation, we were both typing frantically, we caught up on so many areas and shared where our lives had taken us over the last twenty years, the 'good and not so good' and then...Dhush told me about his experiences with Cancer. I felt heartbroken and cried heavily whilst typing (I was glad he could not hear or see me) to know that a dear friend had suffered so much, yet survived such a harrowing time is unimaginable. Dhush wrote so positively and I received it so negatively. I knew this was wrong, but my head was shocked and my heart grieved a time I felt I could have been praying for my friend.

I've heard the phrase "a friend can be a blessing or a lesson" and Dhush epitomizes both!!! He's the devoted friend, the philosopher, the analyst, with a whirlwind of experience and an all-round fabulous person always guiding. Some people just come into your life and make it so much better, like the stars above, they're always there, you just can't always see them because of time or distance, yet our wonderful memories (and in recent times, our Reunion) together with modern technology, we are never really far apart.

Nothing makes me smile more than real love. My family and friends are very real and very dear to me. To have a friend with so much determination and soul, to admire them for their courage and honesty, makes me feel incredibly humble and proud... I thank you Dhush, for your ongoing friendship and memories and for sharing so much of your Self. Your strength and humility are to be admired, plus, you just make me smile.... and, of course "Magic Happens When You Smile"

Love, Marcia O'Keefe (Downes)

For a beautiful person we know…….
our brother Dhush Kuladeva.

By Daljit and Geetha Sedeora

"Believe….and keep going."

Dhushiyantha Kuladeva or Dhush as he is fondly known by everyone was obviously already in my life even before I was born, being my elder cousin from my maternal side (my mother's sister's eldest child). As we were 9 years apart in age, quite expectedly when I was younger he was closer to my siblings and not me, much to my annoyance. As one grows older we realise that age has no barrier to being able to bond with a person and it is more of sharing the same values and attitude to life that brings people closer. This is how I pretty much got closer to Dhush and got to know him more. To be perfectly honest and brutal as one may see it, we got closer when he was first diagnosed with cancer. I remember driving on my own in my first car (a Proton Iswara) all the way from Kuala Lumpur to Johor Bahru and then to Singapore (with Priya, Dhush's sister) to see Dhush in his worst. It broke my heart then and still does every time I think about it. I remember him being bedridden yet so excited to see me and was just so astonished that I had driven all the way on my own to see him. His enthusiasm at that moment just caught me by surprise and I felt all my fear of adventuring on my own from Kuala Lumpur to Johor Bahru was well worth it by just seeing that smile on his face. Here was a guy battling most probably with the worst pain in his life but still had a big smile on his face and there was me fearing the worst about driving solo cross country. It was not even comparable to say the least. I realized from that day forward nothing can defeat you unless you let it. Dhush you are my HERO!!

I got busy with life after that, with work and then came my marriage to Daljit (my soul mate, my best friend, my lover, my husband, the father of my beautiful two girls Shayna and Divyana). I feel compelled to introduce Daljit before I go further as Dhush (Brother D as how Daljit refers to him) has grown to know him and also is rather fond of him if I may say so. I'm not too sure whether we are worthy of being compared to the epics of "Ramayana" but Daljit's and my journey to being husband and wife did not come easy. Daljit and I, having come from different backgrounds did not have it easy and due to this we had to go separate ways after just being together for 6 months due to external factors. Thankfully I have a supportive family (my late dad, mum, two sisters and a brother) who kept telling me if a person is meant to be with you, they will come back into your life. After a silent spell of about a year and a half Daljit tried to get in contact with me again (bear in mind that I had changed my number by this time). Luckily or should I say strangely, he had my mum's number and with an initial seven second call to many calls after that, with poems and flowers left at my front gate daily for a period of 6 moths over, we are now happily married for 13 and half years with two beautiful princesses to account for. I guess Dhush, you are right, even when you were sick you taught me never to give up on things. I can't imagine my world now without Daljit.

We caught up with Dhush on a more regular basis after this when he had a brief stint in Kuala Lumpur and then we also went up to Vietnam to catch up with him on his own turf and realized how amazing a person he is not to have given up on life but to have made himself a truly enriched life despite his illness. We took a big leap in our lives to move to Australia in 2013 in search of a better quality life for us and the kids after being in Malaysia for 40 years and Dhush paid us a visit in August last year. It was wonderful to see him again as having family over is always looked forward upon. Seeing him and Rose (his absolutely beautiful wife) again was lovely and most importantly just seeing him being so happy with life despite being ill, is such a breath of fresh air. It just makes one think that if we always allow life's downs to get us, we would not live, as a life without ups and downs is a life which has not been lived.

Dhush, you are always on our mind with everything that you have gone through. As the old saying goes, "what doesn't kill us only makes us stronger," we have always believed in your ability to overcome any obstacles life may bring. We know that you have had challenges but we want you to know that we have always been there and always will be here for you. We know it is the hardest thing in the world to have to face life being ill but you are a survivor and we always knew you will be alright.

Dhush, focus on the wonderful memories that you have made. Nothing can ever take those from you, ever. You are an inspiration to all who know you and we are honoured to call you our brother, cousin, friend. Be thankful for the life you live and know that you have had a wonderful impact on those around you.

Dhush, please know that we love you with all our hearts and our lives have been enriched having you in it. We are blessed to have you in our lives every day. You are an amazing person to know and to be with; a truly respected gentleman with the warmest heart. We have no doubt that you will go on to touch more lives with each passing day. Be encouraged today our brother, we are so proud of you and the success you have made out of your life and always know that we are always here for you if you need us for anything.

"Take time to be thankful for everything that you have, you can always have more but you could also have less."

Thank you Dhush, for giving us this opportunity to pen down these few words; it's truly a humbling experience and we are eternally grateful for your love and kindness shown to us throughout the years. We cannot believe that you hold us so high in your esteem when quite truthfully, you are the champion in our hearts and you are the one that truly is an inspiration to us and many out there.

Warm hugs always-Daljit and Geetha

Geetha and I at a family function in Malaysia.

A special contribution: By Colleen Randall

The years have drifted by so quickly and life as it was is an intermittent mish-mash of recollections. Dhush says we met on the bus out to Uni but my earliest and most indelible memory is of him dancing. I saw him on the dance floor at the disco above the old Tatts hotel. 'Zandies' the disco was called. The pub isn't there anymore; it was knocked down and replaced with a McDonald's restaurant...an indication of the passage of time from then to now. It was 1985 and I was six months out of high school; raw and naive as a country girl first out of home can be. He moved with a grace and confidence that I had never seen before. I was mesmerised. Having come from Hamilton, the concept of anything as suave as him was remote, to say the least. He seemed so very comfortable within his skin that I couldn't help but be drawn to him. And that smile!! So confident!

He was living with Aiyaz Khaiyum and Reggie when I first met him and their house was party central. In fact most student houses were party central. It just so happened that when our houses joined, we met, and a lifelong friendship was born. There was nothing grandiose about the way we all lived then. As students everything was sparse and economical but our one extravagance was alcohol, oh and cigarettes too, in abundant supply. We came together with the exuberance of adolescence and made the absolute best of the situation, picking and choosing from those with whom we found common ground. Some stayed and some were left behind, but a man like Dhush is not one you let go lightly. There was an honesty and earthiness to him that was surprising and exhilarating too. He accepted people for who they were, and for me, that was unexpected; refreshingly so. I don't remember what we talked about or planned or even what we did, but we were comfortable to be with each other and that is enough for anyone.

Drinking was a large part of our student culture, I say 'our' because there were, apparently, people who were studying who took their dedication to study quite seriously. I can't say that I was one of those people. And, quite frankly, I don't think anyone else I was associated with was either. That's not to say that we didn't do the work required, in fact, the subjects in Social Science were interesting and quite diverting, but there was always practical work to be done and the pub seemed like a good place to put our newly acquired knowledge to use. Our 'major' was laughingly referred to as 'Cafe Studies,' and in hindsight we may have learned more looking and engaging with the people in the cafeteria at College than we did in the classroom. Relationships were important, and hooking up with the right people, those who made you feel extraordinary, was an integral part of the whole Uni-growth-adolescent thing. Dhush was the sort of person who made me feel like that. He had a zest for life that pulsated, like the rhythms that we danced to, he exuded charisma and vivaciousness.

It was the start of the second semester of second year when our relationship was really cemented. I had just moved into a huntsman infested flat in Warrnambool and we were the only two of our crew who had yet returned. It was about that time that Dhush's father had died and he had come back to Australia early. We spent the days just hanging out together and talking (and drinking,) establishing an organic relationship that didn't rely on artifice. It couldn't, the emotion was too raw and the vulnerability too great. I had not seen Dhush anything but happy and buoyant up to that point, and the things we shared brought about a new level of intimacy. Our relationship became more trusting and transparent. We expected nothing less from each other. When we spoke it was honest and heartfelt. He was a patient man and slow to anger but could absolutely go off like a rocket if he was crossed. Thankfully I didn't see much of that.

Dhush was working at the Malaysian Restaurant in town during our college years. We would go out for dinner when finances permitted and he would suggest foods to try - what was good and what wasn't. Our friend Marse always wanted something hot and, with a twinkle in his eye, he'd suggest a meal for her. The results were always hilarious as Marse ate and ate and gradually turned an interesting shade of cerise, sweat emanating from every pore of her face. But she loved it! I hadn't tried Malaysian food before meeting Dhush. My step-mother's idea of Asian cuisine was a jar of Kan Tong, so the extraordinary dining experiences that Dhush introduced me to were marvellous. My palate was stimulated by many different flavours and they remain still a favoured choice of cuisine.

When second year exams were over the relief was palpable and to celebrate Dhush, Marse, our friend Matt and Myself decided a drinking challenge would be a good way to celebrate. I'd known Dhush to be a big drinker and to be able to hold it well. Being a country girl I could also hold my own but this episode proved to be an experience that is forever etched in my memory. We each bought a bottle of Stones Mac (green ginger wine laced with scotch) and settled into the kitchen at Kepler Street to see who could finish their bottle first. There was much laughter and mirth as we each succumbed to inebriation and, of course, Dhush was the first to finish. I believe I was second but spending the next few hours wrapped around the toilet bowl might negate that result. While I was all pasty and horrid, Dhush and Co thought going out would be a good idea. There was no way I could have walked, let alone drank anymore, so they went off and had a great night. As I lay in bed that night watching the room spinning round and round, I was convinced that Dhush had a cast iron stomach and could handle anything. It appears the ensuing years have indeed proven it so. His resilience and strength of character are attributes I have long admired. Needless to say the smell of Stones Mac to this day makes me retch. And one day I may wave a bottle of it under Dhush's nose just to see his reaction. ☺

Acknowledgements

This book is dedicated to my beloved wife Rozana (Rose), who at the most difficult time of my life, stood by me and agreed to marry me. To my mother Punithavathy Vallipuram, the silent force behind my existence on earth, who at 80, still never fails to amaze me, my brother Rajiv, whose encouragement and wisdom and not to mention a great source of philosophical inspiration, spurred me on to embark on this project, my sister Priya Darshini, the pillar of strength and who has been kicking ass with her two brothers and whose zest for nature and its existence has taken on a renewed dimension and my brother in-law Ruben, whose no nonsense to life made it possible for me to cut through the *"waffle"* and get to the point of matter.

To my best friends Shanti Jacqueline and her husband Michael Derrek, your friendship means a great deal to me and both of you have been tremendously instrumental in my quest towards overcoming the challenges that I have faced in life and I'm forever grateful for your invaluable love and support.

To my dearest friends and university family in Warrnambool, Australia where I really grew up and came to realize the meaning of my existence, Colleen Randall, Marcia Jayne Downes, Maria Katselos, Mathew Nolan, Louise Dridan, The late Alistair

Waddleton, just to name a few, your friendship and guidance throughout my years in University can only be viewed as priceless.

I wasn't very articulate in my student years. I had to write everything down and studying for exams was as daunting as asking a woman out on a first date. Absorbing information needed to be based on interactive experiences and actions, while understanding the theory and principles of "cause and effect" enabled me to come up with alternative, yet meaningful answers to life's questions.

The journey into searching for answers and to make sense of my life began with this simple but relatively powerful revelation. The fact that we are all here doing whatever it is that we are doing, tells me that the primal instinct in us is a very real and a justifiable component of our existence. I'm not examining its relevance but simply attempting to place its subliminal within a sphere of basic understanding. I believe that we have managed to maintain an unbroken blood line, and this lineage exists below the threshold of sensation or consciousness, perceived by or affecting our mind without being aware of it. Deep within our soul and even in our sleep like state, we are registering.........

It has been said that those who can't do teach, those who can't teach write! I'm the sort of person who values instinctual decision making and this is my attempt to do both, teach and write. As a student of Psychology and later on as a practitioner for a brief period, it demonstrated that our minds are actually constructed by a myriad of interactions very early in life. Besides a genetic link to our behavioural patterns and to an extent exposure to certain teachings, these early experiences somewhat shape and create the directions of the thought process. I have come to realize that due to a particular regime, rigorous at times, during my early development, this created a solid impact on my existence and of those in my inner circle.

A special mention goes out to my work family in Singapore, Hassan's Carpets. All of you stood by me from the onset of my first diagnosis in 1995. To Athar Hamid and your incredibly warm family, I thank you from the bottom of my heart for taking me and my mother into your home while I underwent radiation therapy. To Neelofur Hamid, your love and support as an elder sister was immeasurable. While I will never be able to repay all of you for your undying support and encouragement, rest assured that I hold all of you in the highest regard and on a pedestal few would be able to scale.

To my second family in Vietnam, my incredible Team at The Gallery Exclusive, I thank you all for putting up with my outbursts, explosion of ideas that made no sense, but we still prevailed in our quest to keep the business alive. I thank you for allowing me the time to get away every so often to work on this book while you took over minding the fort. My sincere gratitude goes out to Anna Dang Thanh Truc, my esteemed colleague, for coming into my life at the most critical moment and having stayed the course to this day.

I've also been blessed to have a wonderful crew of cousins, nephews and nieces. The sheer size of the family and its noticeable extension would mean that mentioning all of them would require another book. However, I would like to express my sincere gratitude to my cousin Geetha Santhira Thesan and her most amazing husband Daljit Singh. This is a couple whose roots can be said to be embedded deep in the epics of The Ramayana, for their love story beckons nostalgia on an entirely new platform. They were incredibly supportive during the years of my personal turmoil and became tremendously instrumental in my journey while I was doing a short business stint in Kuala Lumpur, Malaysia. To the two of you, your undying love and admiration for the simplest things in life and for family values has certainly created a sense of awareness that would leave many in awe.

Finally, this book is especially for my late father Kuladeva Kularatnam. In memory of watching him take his last breath in 1985 woke up an instinctive side in me, and has kept things in perspective ever since. I will never be half the man you were, but I will proudly carry your name.

My parents – on their wedding day

Author's brief

The audacity of survival is about a twenty year battle with Stage four Rectum Cancer. Subsequently, my love for the Art of Oriental Rugs and the journey that followed enabled me to embark on an audacious mission, breaking practically every rule in the book, only to have arrived at this particular juncture. This surreal journey transcends, transports, and catapults my thought process and ideologies of not only surviving but really living life and encapsulates the opulent experience into a phenomenon best described as "euphoric".

This account was initially documented in 2011 with an outline of grave indecisiveness, perhaps due to many external circumstances and internal conflicts within the walls that I seem to have built around me. Then it took a different turn as I came to realize that the art of living was not outlined in a book, neither was it based on a set of rules, trials and tribulations. It was about just getting it done! This meant that I was willing to do things differently, risks and all, the whole nine yards so to speak and I simply wanted to be a survivor of extraordinary audacity. The thought of this was just a small portion of my existence – I already knew that. In some aspects, my approach to life may have been viewed as rude and impertinent, presumptuous and often with great temerity to test the boundaries of fate.

Sidney Poitier's writings influenced me a great deal and in his account of "The Measure of a Man", he writes; *"from the succession of excellent objects, we learn at last the immensity of the world, the opulence of human nature, which can run out to infinitude in any direction"* made me realize that the self cannot be developed – everything is a process of growth. It was internal disharmony that resulted in infecting everything around me with misery and conflict. Joy was not happening within me and core humanity was not functioning. Something needed to change. I needed to function cohesively with my mind and to test its uniqueness meant removing the "box". I simply needed to work upon myself and treat cancer as a part of my life's daily path.

This soulful account is a result of my having given the last twenty years of my life numerous opportunities to change its course and yet, it never did happen. It wasn't necessary. I was not in a competition anymore and I realized that the end could very well be the beginning. Inadvertently this version of my language, my speech on life was not a matter of concern. I was more interested in the science of art and education. It was about my personal development and I took it upon myself to look at this experience as a reasonable discourse that eventually sealed the process of path finding.

I know that I will never reach the peak, my zenith, but this will not stop me from experiencing euphoria – the opulent and audacious experience. Touching on my illness and my passion for the "arts" collectively may seem to be an unusual marriage of ideals but it worked. This book will reveal the path that I have taken and hopefully shed some light into this immense thirst for life that has gripped my sheer existence, my refusal to give in, to give up and to thrive on the infectious spirit of belonging intrinsically to existence.

My brother has reminded me repeatedly that this book should be a gathering of my thoughts and not a collection of theories and my sister has eloquently mentioned that as long as it's internal, I already have a best seller. I will try to stay on course and do both, not only for my present generation but for the generations to come.

Thank you for reading and enjoy the journey ahead.

1

Orientalism- The Opulence of the East

"You may be treading on a work of art without knowing it"

The year was 1987, and as a graduating student with a degree in the Social Sciences, my views on philosophy, sociology and psychology were fresh. I was ready to be engaged in the conundrum of the real world. It was two years after losing my father to cancer and it had been a tumultuous journey for the family. My mother was living in Adelaide at that time, together with my brother, who was pursuing his passion and degree in architecture. My sister was in high school. As a family, we had always wanted to live in the West, and Australia was an attraction then.

It was way back in the early 1970's when my father was offered an opportunity to immigrate to Australia as it was a period when qualified English teachers were very much in demand. True to his ways, he said there would be no one to look after his mother, my grandmother who later passed on, also due to cancer. I never met my paternal grandfather, Kularatnam, but from what I have been told, he was a strict disciplinarian. At the age of thirty nine, he left his family, as he was called to be with the Lord, leaving behind nine children. Cancer had struck again, so you can imagine the toll this must have taken on my father, who lost his dad when he was just fourteen years old.

I was fortunate enough to have gained entry into an Australian university and went on to pursue a degree in Warrnambool, Victoria. This was the place that shaped my views on life and independence and stamped my love for rugs. I'll elaborate more on Warrnambool and the incredible five years that I had spent with new friends, later on in this journey. For now, let me take you back to 1987. Melbourne was a trendy city, filled with bars, cafes, and fashion boutiques. Walking down High Street in Armadale was the thing to do, people of all ages would gather in their favourite haunts, and it never seemed to lose its appeal. Toorak, South Yarra was not far away so this belt was one I would patronise almost daily. I remember this particular day in April, I had just finished my exams and was going into my elective year, which meant I had more time to do something other than study and cook pizzas as a part-time job. Little did I realise that this would be the most meaningful and significant day of my life, one that would have created such a defined and profound impression on the labour of love.

I was walking past a trendy strip on High Street and came across a carpet shop, well more like a boutique. Its façade was of French influence, and it was a sprawling space, decked out with some of the most breathtakingly beautiful rugs and ornaments. There, on the wall, behind the unassuming reception desk, was a carpet hanging within an enclosed brass frame. It looked old, with muted gold and bronze colours but with a design that blossomed from the bottom of the earth. The fellow at the front desk looked up and invited me into his shop. Hesitantly I entered, and even before saying anything else, I asked the most ridiculous question, "Is this carpet machine-made? How much is it?"

He was silent for a moment and glared at me. Then he took a deep puff from his cigarette and let out a huge "sigh"! I thought, *that's it, I am 'screwed' now!* Still, the arrogance in me prevailed, and I was steadfast in my reaction, – cool and calculated. I waited patiently and was getting ready to walk out when I noticed a book on carpets on the table: *The Persian Rug* by A. Cecil Edwards. I'd seen this book before, and in those days, we actually spent a lot of time reading, since there was no Internet.

Finally, a voice broke from the silence and I was invited to sit down. We exchanged pleasantries for a moment, and then there was silence again. I couldn't help being totally consumed by the aura of anticipation in this place – it was magical. We could have just sat there for hours, doing nothing, but it would have been awkward, to say the least. He picked up the book and mentioned that it was his daily companion. I asked if I could flip through the book, and he said, "No no!"-He proceeded to point me in the direction of the very first article that was embedded in between the pages.

It looked like a torn-out page from another publication. It read, "Art of the Woven Legend" and featured in front were designs by William Morris. If you are familiar with *Architectural Digest* in the late '80'-s William Morris was a regular contributor to the art of carpet designs. He writes: *"To give people pleasure in the things they must perforce use that is one great decoration. To give people pleasure in the things that they must perforce make that is the other use of it."* This was, to me, an unfinished sentence. I couldn't make head or tail of it.

I mean, what was the big deal? During this time, the chap at the front desk, who was a Kashmiri living in Melbourne, was quietly observing my reaction to this somewhat debilitating dilemma and offered to make sense of it all. He said, "Infinity"- There are no rules to follow. I was still not getting it!

He begged for my indulgence, as I was getting irritated with his delaying tactics. I just wanted to know if the carpet was machine-made and the price. I didn't ask for a god- damn lecture. Nevertheless, I was curious. We were starting to bond rather unexpectedly and he asked me to read the first chapter from another publication, – *The Hali Magazine,* – the international publication on art and textiles. Bear with me here and I'll tell you in a moment how all this changed my perspective on 'rugs". The opening reads:-

"The abyss between the old and new was explained in rainforest language of rarity and distinction. It was a view that divided the world, east and west into sellers of dowries and sellers of estates with everyone brokering their way through. It was folklore built on the backs of the folk, who were rumoured to trade old rugs for machinery and grain bags for household items. At one point, looking into a shop window at any rug, new or old that passed for quality, who were we to argue against the final outcome? The litany of loss was universal and evoked the names of the people from particular tribes, trading centres and prominent weaving master workshops. Who then could say that, art and commerce had not lost their footing and direction when The Oriental Carpet collided with the 21st century?"

I was even more lost now than before, and after reading this over and over again, the message was finally beginning to unfold. I understood it to mean that the opulence of the East was a remarkable discovery, and art lovers, traders or brokers could see beyond the realm of commercialism when dealing with the wonders of the Oriental carpet. It didn't matter where the carpet was from or how much it was–: what it meant was that the ingenuity of the weavers and their dedication proved to be invaluable proponents of infinite possibilities.

The abyss, – the endless continuation in design and message between the old and new, was rare, and it was explained in simple language – purity and simplicity in its highest form. I asked myself, how can something so elaborate be considered simple? Undoubtedly, I could see the purity in its representation. I was hooked on this subject matter and more so, the carpet that was still hanging on the wall. An Australian-currency $4,000 price tag was revealed to me for the carpet in question, and my Kashmiri friend referred to it as a hand knotted rug. I loved the arrogance in him: - in the way he would manipulate all possibilities of conjuring up a story, – any story to describe that rug. He wasn't trying to sell me the rug. I couldn't afford the price tag anyway but could not pass up the offer to work for him.

This was the beginning of a love affair far and beyond. To be certain, I made it clear that I was not taking the job offer just to look good in a suit and tie. I needed a job, but I was not expecting this. However, I needed to be part of this experience. I wondered what my family would think of me being a sales-person, when all the other cousins were doctors, lawyers and engineers! I was twenty three years old then and wanted to learn to have the gift of the gab, as did my Kashmiri friend. I was totally consumed by his eloquence and knowledge of the trade and in the art-form. We exchanged contact details, and before I left, he stood up and said *"Chalo bhai"*. – Okay, brother, tomorrow you will start work in the warehouse. Your job will be to open up the bales from new shipments, clean up the floor and help to stack all the bales - And you will be operating a forklift!

What the hell?! "What happened to the suit and tie?" I asked!

He smiled at me and said, "Time will tell. Now- you will have to be patient and work your way up". Before I left, he presented me with *The Persian Carpet* by Cecil Edwards and told me to treat this as my carpet bible.

I thanked my friend and my new boss and left. I couldn't wait to start work, to open up the bales, just to see what treasures were in each package. I still have Cecil Edward's book on my book shelf and each time I look at the images of the "rugs" in the pages, totally consumed by the plethora of motifs and colours, it reminds me of an orchestra – the balance of flora and fauna appearing so natural, the tune in perfect harmony. All this was referred to as The Opulence of the East and I was consumed by the word. While planning the opening chapter of this book, I sent a 'WhatsApp' message to my sister who cleverly said "Opulent means rich and superior in quality". I wanted this to be my life, my mission and my purpose. This was going to be my mantra in life. For the next two decades and more, the word opulence shaped my life and helped me through the most difficult times when I was struck down with cancer. I turned to "rug art" and the intensity of colour and motifs for therapy. In the book by Cecil Edwards, he mentions that "the alchemy of weave, colour and design in beautiful rugs is tied to one's visceral response to materials, to palette and fleece". It is the hierarchy that binds the minds' eye to a drop spindle and a copper cauldron, echoing times when guilds existed and whole communities centred on the making of art. I was completely consumed by the insatiable thirst to know more about this magnificent creation which was loosely referred to as a "rug".

All throughout my time as a rug dealer in Melbourne and until I left Australia in early 1989, this art-form kept me in constant contact with a Company called "Hassan's". This was a name that appeared on all the bales that I used to open in the warehouse. From the warehouse, I steadily progressed to be part of the Exhibition Team, travelling throughout Australia organizing road shows and events. This was exactly what I needed and after graduating, I needed to break away to keep me steady in the course of each day. I was the guy who would yearn for something different and not to mention audacious. I was the guy that would eventually elevate my ability to interact with people from all walks of life. I was the guy that would break all the rules of engagement, especially within the family context and in the world of business.

By the way, in case you were wondering, I did purchase that "rug" on the wall. It was an exquisite hand-knotted 100% pure silk Turkish Hereke with a Tree of Life design. It measured 5ft x 3ft.

Naturally, I paid a whole lot less than the asking price.

2

Serendipity – Journey to Singapore

"When applying collective unconscious to collective consciousness, something unexpected transpires"

Everything happens for a reason, or as "karma" personifies, as the result of cause and effect. All throughout my short stint as a "rug dealer" in Australia, I learned to navigate through the landscape of business and social interactions. The trade taught me to appreciate the clarity of thought in the various categories of rugs that I had handled while conforming to the kaleidoscope of colour and brilliance in shades. The artistic invasion was embedded in my personal psyche and I left the business with an aura of anticipation, not knowing if I was ever going to be in this line of work again. Soon, it was time to leave Australia, my visa had run out and like all Malaysian students before me, the idea was to travel to New Zealand for a brief period, get a job and then make my way back to Australia as a visitor or as a possible applicant in a professional capacity. I had already been to New Zealand once before and visited Auckland, Wellington and Dunedin, even managing to squeeze in some cross country skiing at one point.

This was a poignant moment for me since I was free from the clutches of a routine life as a student, and I was indeed hopeful of finding a suitable position to begin my career. Naturally, with limited funds, I stayed at the YMCA in Auckland and distinctively remember my very first night in a 7 x 4ft room, the single bed edged into a corner and a tiny view of the city from the obscure window above the study table. That was the first time that I had actually cried, not from being alone, but from the fear of dying in this hell hole. Thinking back, it wasn't that bad, however, I was used to living in a huge mansion in Melbourne which I had shared with a group of friends and to find myself in this tiny space but just too overwhelming. Still, I sucked it all in and told myself to '*cut the crap*' and do what I had come here to do – to find a job.

The plan was to stay in New Zealand for a month or so and I found my way around Auckland with relative ease. Hope, relief, and a new kind of sadness that I was struggling with turned to an unexpected discovery. I found that recent graduates from Australia were given priority to apply for permanent residence status in New Zealand if they were successful in obtaining suitable employment. This meant that if a particular position that was available could not be filled by a native New Zealander, then I stood a chance. I frantically started applying for jobs in all areas of work. I looked at various positions in the social services industry, counselling, journalism, and soon realized that it wasn't as easy as everyone had made it out to be. The local library was a regular meeting point and since I was a sociable fellow, making new friends was never an issue. My group of friends grew steadily and I soon found myself patronizing the local pubs while working part time in the local milk bars as a helping hand, and even tried selling groceries in a '*fruit and veggie*' shop. I did what I needed to do to keep myself busy and earn a little money. The native Maoris were not a friendly bunch as they looked at any dark Asians as Islanders. They hated the Fijians and anyone from Papua New Guinea and I soon found myself being labelled as one of them. The treatment was harsh, we couldn't get our daily dose of milk and bread or sausage rolls for breakfast and I was not a happy man. This was not going according to plan and after almost a month of living in New Zealand, I decided that this would be a good time to return to Australia. My mother was still in Adelaide then and I knew that she was already making plans to return to Malaysia. If memory serves me right, my sister was living with my brother and some friends in Adelaide and since they seemed settled, my mother felt that it was probably the right time to return home to Malaysia.

I went ahead to the Australian Immigration Office in Auckland and put in my application for a tourist visa to Australia, and mentioned on the application form that I was intending to visit my mother, and we would both be returning to Malaysia. Subconsciously, I really had no intentions of returning to Malaysia. It was the late '80's and Malaysia had just come out of recession so I knew for a fact that I would probably be paid pittance if I were to work at home. Some of my friends who had left university prior to this had already secured their first entry level jobs and were earning a miserable Malaysian-currency $500 to $600. Back then, this was 'small money', but enough for one to get by if they were living at home with their parents, save a little and after some time, show off their first proton saga – the Malaysian made car. I was already earning a whole lot more, and in New Zealand Dollars, doing odd jobs so this didn't make sense to me.

Deep down, the thought of returning home was not on the priority list. You see, at that time, if you were studying and living abroad, they idea was to stay put and find a job overseas, get married to a foreigner and live a life that would apparently be the envy of your friends and relatives. I confidently put in my application and to my utter surprise and dismay, it was rejected. I was bloody livid! How could they do this to me? I marched right up to the immigration officer and voiced out my dissatisfaction, to which she vehemently said, "sorry"! Not approved. I was adamant and so was she and in the end, I had no choice but to give in and accept the decision. I was hopeful as I left the immigration office and thought that I'd wait a few days before letting my mother know what was going on.

Later that night, in my cubicle and after 'polishing off a six pack', I began searching into the empty space in my consciousness which was already getting 'smashed' on alcohol together with what could have been a relentless act of chain smoking. I eventually drifted off into a deep sleep while strangely being conscious of what had transpired the day before. I was very upset with the universe and everyone else around me. I remembered my training in psychology and some literature that I had read on the advances in the human condition and reflected upon the fact that our entire universe is contained in the mind and spirit. We may decide not to access it and we may even come up with a thousand and one theories denying its existence, but it is indeed there, inside us.

This was a huge let down and I looked at it as a situation of turmoil and frustration. I even considered detaching myself from humanity. I was, for a considerable period, someone who could not take rejection well. I needed to belong, I needed re affirmation and I so desperately needed to be recognized. I told myself that I had already obtained a degree and this was a huge achievement considering the fact that my leaving certificate grades (Form Five) were dismal on all fronts. I obtained a Grade Two with just one distinction, while I had cousins and siblings who had aced their exams. So this degree was actually aimed at everyone around me and although it was not a degree in medicine or law, to me, it was priceless. And so began the decision to stop sulking. I picked myself up from the pathetic state that I had put myself in just because I was denied entry into Australia. It was time to claim my life back and get out of this hell hole-it was time for the prodigal son to return home. My sister will still attest to this affirmatively that when it comes to me, I'm still the prodigal son. 'Go figure'!

With all enthusiasm and a positive outlook, I rang home to tell everyone that I was leaving New Zealand, and that I was returning home. I wasn't sure if there was a frenzy of excitement back home upon hearing the news, but I could sense it, and the feeling of apprehension was slowly fading. Despite my ambiguous intentions, I knew deep down that I needed to get my act together, after all I was twenty four years old, and it was time for me to help with the family expenses and not forgetting the fact that I still had two younger siblings who needed to complete their education overseas. As a Ceylonese from Malaysia, our only choice of a valued education was an overseas one. It was a known fact.

I despise admitting to failure. I was coming to terms with the fact that the great Australian dream had not materialized, and it somewhat left me naked in my immediate surroundings. Although I was now in my home country, my mother did not have a home. You see, after my father's demise, my mother decided to sell the house in order to have some money set aside in case my brother or sister needed it. It also helped with my last few years in university to a small extent, while I supported myself on the whole, working full time.

So I was now in my home town where I grew up. This is Seremban, a small town which by then was already a municipality. The town had expanded quite rapidly and it was also becoming congested. I was, nonetheless unemployed, and living with my uncle and his family in my maternal grandfather's home was a welcoming thought. Both my maternal grandparents were alive then, although my grandfather was already getting on with age, - pushing ninety. When my father had passed on and after a few more younger relatives went in similar fashion, my grandfather decided that he had lived long enough and decided to go on a hunger strike. I think he wanted to break Mahatma Ghandi's record, so at the time of my grand return home, while still lucid, grandfather was slowly ailing. My grandmother was still as healthy as ever, although past history would indicate that she had suffered a heart attack sometime back. I was really given a hero's welcome and I probably had the best few months of my life, living care free for that brief period. Nevertheless, the mere thought of still being unemployed created shortcomings and feelings of vulnerability and inadequacy. I was consumed, once again, by an insurmountable feeling of self-doubt and uselessness. I was really burdened by the look of worry on my mother's face, whose daily doses of "it's time for you to get a job" was in plain-sight. I had to 'get off my arse'.

Strangely, this was the time that marriage proposals started pouring in, thanks to my beloved grandmother who had secretly been plotting a plan to get me married off to the daughter of their close family friend. My grandmother held very strong beliefs that I would not have a problem agreeing to this arrangement. She had an innate sense of power within the family circle and in fact, it was at this time I was informed that it was my grandmother who had convinced my father not to allow me to enter into cadet flying school with the Royal Malaysian Air Force – something that I had always dreamt of doing while in school. She forbade it and my father at the time said "no"! So you see, grandmother was a formidable force in the family.

Needless to say, it was time for me to make my move and do everything in my power to get a job. I had to achieve this viscerally, instinctively and in some strange way, spiritually. There was no turning back. I wasn't about to be married off! This was not the time for me to do this, as I was just twenty four years old and was in no hurry to settle down. Settling down almost happened in Australia when I was about to marry a long-time girlfriend and being Australian and all that, it was an exciting proposition, for me personally. However, as fate would have it, this was not meant to be. After another month or so of soul searching and attending ridiculous interviews in Kuala Lumpur, where the basic and starting salary for a research officer was Malaysian-currency $500, then this was about American-currency 120 per month, I decided that this was not up to my standards. With my appetite for life, this wouldn't have lasted one week.

As chance would have it, my good friend Raj, who had worked with me in the carpet boutique in Melbourne back in 1987, was already in Singapore and he was with a firm called Hassan's Carpets. I remembered this name, as I recalled the many carpet bales that I had opened up in the warehouse during my first few months as a rug merchant. Raj mentioned that there was an opening for a sales position in Singapore and asked if I was interested. I was excited at the prospect of working abroad again, although Singapore was just a stones' throw away from Malaysia, it was still considered overseas. I had my passport validated, and applied for a restricted passport which back then, was the document that everyone used to travel between Malaysia and Singapore. I was invited for an interview in Kuala Lumpur's

Hilton Hotel and met with an impressionable chap by the name of Abdul Rahman Talib. He was a class act, tall, with a prominent moustache and walked upright with his Dunhill briefcase and cigarette hanging off his lower lip.

Rahman and I spoke for a brief moment and we had dinner to discuss the employment options. However I remember that we spoke very little about the business or the job but more about his conquests in Hilton! Obviously a 'player' at that time, I was once again taken in with the lifestyle of the opulent and successful. I could see myself prancing around five-star hotel lobbies, sipping champagne and smoking branded cigarettes. My mind was made up and I decided to accept the job offer in Singapore. I left the interview with a sense of relief and went home to my uncle's house. Later that night, I telephoned my mother to tell her that I had secured a job in Singapore. She asked me about the job and when she heard that it was a sales position, I could hear the disappointment in her silence over the phone. I mentioned that this was probably for the best and the money was a whole lot better than the dismal offers that I was receiving from the companies in Malaysia.

Subconsciously, I never expected to be going back into the "rug" business but this was fate. A fortuitous happenstance and as luck would have it, this unexpected interview turned out to be a decision of a lifetime. The journey to Singapore was confirmed and after buying a third class train ticket, the prodigal son had once again, left home for greener pastures. I had arrived at a certain juncture in my life, surrounded by certain circumstances and in one deciding moment, the entire journey had come to life. Serendipity perhaps!

3

Birth of the Business Man

"Where thy carpet lies is thy kingdom"

Right about the time of my departure from my home-town -
Seremban, my brother and sister had received the news that I had
accepted a job in Singapore. We had no cell phones or emails then
so we often wrote to each other or called on the phone. They
were excited to hear about my new venture. I on the other hand,
was familiar with the teachings of Freud in psychoanalysis, and
remembered a long standing debate about the decisive moments in
our lives. According to Freud, 'the context of discovery is strictly
irrelevant to the context of justification'. We can come to know
the thinker's intellectual style and progressively make out whether
his or her theory tended to be responsive to recalcitrant facts and
to the objects of sceptical challenges. This was indeed a decisive
moment in my life. I packed everything I owned in three suitcases
and headed to Singapore, not knowing where I was going to stay
the night. It wasn't exactly frightening but attesting to the fact that I
was in a heightened state of panic would not be stretching the truth.

As I was approaching Singapore's railway station after clearing
the Malaysian check point, immigration officers came on board

the train to check our travel documents. I was excited and apprehensive at the same time. My good friend Raj had arranged to meet me at the railway station and with my heart beat racing and skipping a beat every so often, the train finally pulled into the Singapore's Tanjong Pagar Railway Station. This was still a colonial building at the time, and it was still owned by the Malaysian Government and the building stood on Malaysian soil, despite being in Singapore. One would immediately recognize the dilapidated condition of the railway station and the public toilets brought back immediate memories that one was still in Malaysia. Still, the air was different – my passport was already stamped to indicate that I was now in Singapore. I was, once again, on foreign soil.

Unknowingly, Raj had completely forgotten that I had changed my travel itinerary and that my train was arriving a lot earlier. There was no sign of him. This was not a big deal and I proceeded to the nearest public phone and called the company. He was apparently busy attending to a customer in the shop and the person I spoke to gave me the address of Tanglin Shopping Centre. I hailed a taxi and was soon on my way. I felt no sense of abandonment as the taxi made its way to the City. I still remember the conversation I had with the driver who asked if I was from India and when I said Malaysia, he wasn't impressed either. Nevertheless, he was polite and spoke briefly about my destination and offered some valuable insights into the best pork and chicken rice stalls. This was valuable information indeed.

The concrete jungle which I was in seemed quite inviting. Everything was in perfect order; even the plants along the road dividers were perfectly manicured. As we drove through the afternoon traffic, I noticed that there were many flats around the city and in the neighbourhood – this reminded me of the low cost flats we had back home in Malaysia. Then we arrived at the much talked about Orchard Road Vicinity and the scenery changed. There were more houses, landed properties, endless shopping stores and hotels, all lined up one after another. It was as if they had been plucked from another world and planted in their respective slots. Tanglin Shopping Centre was an older building and as I was alighting from the taxi, the driver mentioned that this was one of the earliest and oldest shopping centres. I didn't pay much attention to this somewhat irrelevant information as I had three large suitcases to unload. Back then, taxi drivers were not known to get out to help with your baggage, their job was to drive and collect money. I paid the Singapore-currency $12 fare and went about unloading my baggage. There was a security chap in the front of the building, I still remember him, and Tony was his name, with a huge beer belly and tattoos all over his arms. He sprang into action and as he was helping me to carry my stuff up to the entrance, who do I see but Raj! I was so relieved to see a familiar face.

Raj greeted me with a bear hug and we proceeded to walk to the end of the ground floor, while passing antique shops selling furniture and old maps. I was immediately consumed by the environment and was in awe with the surroundings. I'd never seen anything like this before and at the end of the corridor was Hassan's Carpets. This was a carefully selected location as it was situated at the end of the corridor where one would have to pass by to exit the building, and also enter the building if necessary. It was a very strategic location, I thought. The first unusual and noticeable sign at the front of the shop was one which read '786' in Arabic. I wondered what this meant. I went in and introduced myself to the gentleman at the front desk, who was one of the two brothers who was in charge of the business.

I was so enthralled by the interior of the shop that I failed to notice an older gentlemen sitting behind him. He happened to be the owner, Mr Hassan himself. The younger Hassan asked if I wanted a drink to which I obliged and was served instant coffee. I hadn't been exposed to 'espresso' and 'nespresso' was unheard off then, so instant coffee was just fine. What amazed me the most as I looked around was that everyone was smoking in the shop, and it was a carpet shop, filled with very expensive carpets, or should I say "rugs". I was offered a cigarette to which I politely declined out of respect for the older people in there. Little did I realize that this was the 'done thing'! Well, the short introduction to the team was carried out and I then met the older brother who was the master swagger. Both of them had an impression on me. I began to recollect all the information that I had read from my "carpet bible" – *The Persian Carpet by A. Cecil Edwards*. Images of various carpets and their relevant provenance began flashing in my head. Eventually, the younger of the two brothers asked me to join him for a drink in the local coffee joint in the basement – I was pretty certain he could sense that I was gagging for a cigarette!

Camouflage removed; meet Khawaja Athar Hamid, the second in line to this apparently flourishing family run and operated business. Hamid, as he was affectionately known to his friends, gave me his business card which read *"Hassan's Carpets" – Purveyors of Fine Oriental Carpets, 3 Generations of Carpet Expertise*. The card was simple with an embossed logo of a sprouting tree – aptly described as "The Tree of Life" Symbolically; this was somewhat relevant to the very first carpet that I had acquired in Melbourne not too long ago. Hamid was the suave "Omar Khayyam" type persona and dressed immaculately in his tailored clothes, while his intellectual discourse was evidently prominent in the way he spoke English, in his low monotone voice emanating a sense of calm throughout. He didn't seem to have the Singapore slang which I had already been introduced to during my conversation with the taxi driver, the slang which I would describe as an unbelievably profane patois of counter cultural jargon. Hamid exchanged some information about the business and mentioned that the most important element of the job was integrity and honesty. By this time, after spending almost five years of my life on my own, I had come to value certain attributes and traits that were essential and naturally instinctual such as commitment, responsibility, and good old fashioned hard work. I expressed my earnest and deeply rooted desire to succeed and work tirelessly from then on. It went well and I could sense that this man was not only successful but held firm beliefs about value.

I sensed that my mind was metabolizing what I was doing at the time. I started to recall the indispensable years I learned the ways of navigating through various landscapes, both professionally and personally, and thought to myself that this was the right decision. For a young man with sensualist inclinations, Singapore was the perfect getaway. I suppose this was another attempt at my mission in life, to completely manipulate the lonely spot in my inner most being with a new adventure. Prior to this, I had always felt that I had treated the world respectfully and looked at this new chapter of my life as an exciting moment. As a healthy twenty four year old, I was ready to embark on this journey of discovery and into the journey of infinite possibilities.

After smoking a few cigarettes and drinking coffee, Hamid and I went back to the shop to meet with his elder brother Suliman and his father, Mr Asghar Hassan. Suliman had the gift of the gab, he was the man responsible for taking the business into its third generation and although he was familiar with all aspects of the lifestyle of the wealthy, his down to earth disposition would often portray him in his traditional Pakistani costume and slippers. He preferred the purity and simplicity of appreciating his precious assets surrounding him daily, quite unlike his younger brother. We spoke at great length about the business and I knew then that this was an area of concern that would inevitably consume my life. Suliman shared his views and experience about the world of "rugs" and said nonchalantly that the art of seduction and flattery never hurt anyone. He admired the ability in anyone who could cajole a possible customer while handling their request with panache and style. I could see myself doing this- not effortlessly, but with some sense of ease over time. Suliman said that he would teach me about people skills and I knew he would since his interpersonal skills spoke volumes. Reflecting quietly, I could sense that this was the beginning of an opulent experience, rich in style and sophistication. I would be selling "rugs" which at that time were priced at thousands of dollars individually.

The next meeting of the day was with the man himself, Mr Hassan. He was "uncle" to everyone and that was how I greeted him. He was a man of distinction, character and a definite style of sophistication and grace prevailed over his persona. At seventy years of age, "uncle" was a workaholic and was known to be a no-nonsense man, much like a revered elder statesman. Everyone feared him, just quietly. He was the silent one who preferred not to say too much, but nonetheless, was known to have dealt numerous and not to mention, firm verbal blows when it was deemed necessary. "Uncle" welcomed me to the family and we didn't say much thereafter. After a moment of silence, Raj gestured to me that it was time to leave the shop as I was expected to meet another senior member of the firm in another one of its outlets not too far away on Orchard Road. Tabriz Carpets was the sister company and I was going to be spending the next few

years there. As I left, I wondered if I was going to forge a bond
with my prospective employers…

I lugged my three suitcases into the company station wagon and
Raj drove me to Centrepoint – one of the numerous shopping
centres which I had seen on my initial taxi ride into the city.
Along the way, Raj pointed out the "watering holes" and some
great places to eat, all of which seemed rather fancy to me at the
time. Nonetheless, it was promising and I knew that I would
soon be a regular face in some of them. We arrived at Centre
Point's loading bay and parked illegally! The suitcases were lugged
up the trolley and we pushed them up the ramp. After a few
inconspicuous turns, I found myself on the fifth floor and at the
end of the corridor, another strategic location, was Tabriz Carpets.

This was a much smaller outlet, brightly lit with hundreds of rugs
stacked on the floor and hanging on the walls – even along the
lengthy windowed corridor. It was a kaleidoscope of patterns and
motifs, all with a story to tell and I couldn't wait to get in there.
I dumped my bags at the front of the shop and entered to greet
everyone. I noticed, once again, that smoking in the premises
was a done thing and wondered if they were insured! How naïve
of me! We exchanged salutations and next to the reception desk
was a tiny cubicle, which was the office of the senior member
of the family that I was supposed to meet. He heard the small
commotion outside and came out and it was a familiar face. It
was Abdul Rahman Talib, the man who had interviewed me in
Kuala Lumpur. I felt a huge sense of relief almost immediately
and Rahman welcomed me into his room. He commented on the
high rental rates in Singapore and that one could only afford to sit
in a small office. I thought nothing of it though. He asked about
my journey after we had a smoke and an espresso, freshly brewed
from his coffee machine in the back room, we decided to take

a walk around the shopping centre. Now I was impressed. Raj excused himself and said that he would come back for me later. It was already late in the evening then and I wondered what time everyone knocked off work. Apparently business hours were from 11am to 8pm and 11am to 4pm on Sundays. We would have one day off per week. I remember Raj mentioning that taking a day off in this business was unheard off as there is always something to do. He was right!

Rahman was a confident man and he appeared to be wealthier and moved with even more swagger and style than the motley crew that I had met earlier in the day. Naturally, I wanted all of this. I wanted the life. I wanted to wear his Patek Philippe watch. After a brief walk around, we went to the first floor for some Indonesian food. "Sanur Indonesian restaurant" was Rahman's favourite place and he bought me dinner. We chatted extensively and it was then that he mentioned that I would be working under him. My first job was to assist in the restoration and redevelopment of Singapore's quintessential landmark, The Raffles Hotel. My trail blazing journey of minuscule proportions had just taken a new twist and I was about to embark on an amazing and challenging project. Few things get a person more interested in engaging in something profoundly interesting than a dose of excitement. I had to get over the exhilaration and come to terms with the fact that I was now a businessman. I was about to be part of a family business and at the helm were two brothers, their father and this man, Abdul Rahman Talib, and they were backed by a somewhat large entourage of loyal staff. Apparently, everyone who worked with this family had already been there for more than ten years.

I couldn't wait to tell my mother and family about this exciting new opportunity and the circle of people that I would be engaging with. I found myself in a paradox of priority. There were some contradictions within me as to how I was feeling at the time, I was apprehensive and still didn't know where I would be spending the night. Nevertheless, I found myself to be in a state of temporary well-being as I promoted the thought of logically accepting the fact that this new sales job was a valuable one, despite the fact that I had arrived in the business world armed with a degree in the Social Sciences. While I couldn't see the relevance at the time, and wondered if my years of study were a waste of money, I argued internally that time would change its course, and my destiny would soon be clearly defined.

For now, I needed a place to stay and to my great relief, the Hassan's family had already made arrangements for me to stay with their younger brother Imran, whose apartment was a mere five to seven minute walk from Tanglin Shopping Centre. Imran, a bachelor then, had just returned from the United Kingdom and was employed in one of Singapore's prestigious law firms. At the time of my arrival, he was travelling along the silk route, which meant nothing to me at the time. Imran's apartment was filled with rugs, mostly deep in colour and simple in style. There was another person staying there at the time and since my employment contract included accommodation, this was a damn good arrangement. My good friend Raj helped me settle into Belmont Road, one of Singapore's trendiest and most opulent neighbourhoods at the time. Another one of my work colleagues was staying in the apartment below mine and I had a room with an attached bathroom.

The apartment was like a treasure cove, filled with the occupant's personal collection of antiques, ornaments, furniture and not forgetting, 'rugs'. I was totally in love with this place. After unpacking, I took a walk around the estate to familiarize myself with the surroundings and to check out the bus route to centre-point shopping centre. After settling into my new home, I called my mother and uncle in Seremban to tell them that I was still in one piece and that I would be starting work the next day. That was that, and it was time for me to settle in for the night. Imran had a wonderful collection of books and periodicals and not to mention the "carpet bible' – The Persian Carpet. It seemed that Cecil Edwards was everywhere. Naturally, I decided to read a little before going to bed and wrote this down:-

> *"Momentous moments and events occasionally erupt from routine experiences. I seek to explore the endless possibilities of this artful creation, which has been recorded to have preceded the invention of writing. The hand makes seven different movements to tie just one knot – it's like alchemy"*

I couldn't help but feel that while my language may be artless, the masterpieces that I have seen in books and will soon be able to touch will certainly paint a different picture and hopefully expose a new level of appreciation. After all, the power of this magnificent art-form isn't in the accumulation of detail; it is about the labour of love, tied knot by knot. And hanging above my bed was an inscription woven in wool which read: "Where Thy Carpet Lies Is Thy Kingdom"

This was my kingdom!

4

The Tale of Two Stories

"In anticipation of a pending catastrophe, a tsunami of events might not exactly cripple you"

There are certain things or traits that we seem to inherit that don't seem to resonate with others, our parents, siblings, relatives, but eventually they will surface. Is this an inherent fact? It has been said that we are all connected in some way, and that we are closer than you think. A great discovery in mankind may not necessarily be passed down from father to son but I believe that it could have existed in generations before that. This is the developmental process that I was exploring within my psyche and it was all starting to come to life in this new surrounding that I had placed myself in. It was time to allow this environment to examine my past and at the same time, create a new platform of the new experience that I was about to be engaged in. While it may be critically important to examine the past in order to ascertain the present, I'm more of a firm believer in the art of conquest. This was my new mission and I was about to set the path in motion.

Waking up after a good night's rest, I found my "kingdom" to be peaceful and serene, perhaps the countless artefacts and "rugs' surrounding me played a great part in this apparent state of mind. Nevertheless, I couldn't help but feel an immense sense of apprehension at the same time and it was clear that my unconscious mind was going head on with an imminent state of consciousness. It was my very first day of work in Singapore and I was nervous. I needed more time to settle in and to look around before embarking on this new mission. Well, this epic setting and dilemma unfolded into a quick reality check when I heard a loud knock on the door – it was Raj, who seemed to be in a bloody hurry to pick me up and get on with the day. I remember it was about 9am and since the shop would only be opened at 11am, I wondered what the commotion was all about.

It was quickly revealed to me that the morning routine for anyone who took the company car back was to arrive at the Hassan's family home for breakfast. Here, we would be in the company of the grand old lady, Mrs Hassan and her children, and not forgetting old man Hassan himself. Now, the old lady may have been showing signs of age then, but she was by no means a feeble woman. She would insist that everyone sit around the breakfast table and converse before heading out to work. There would be some small talk, but it was the time when only a select few would be given the rare opportunity to bond! I thought to myself that as imposing as it was, I should consider myself fortunate to be treated in such a welcoming manner and enjoyed some home cooked food at the same time. I was shy at the beginning but as time went by, this regular morning routine would come to resonate well with my spirits.

This was 1989, and the economy was nursing its wounds from the 1987 financial crisis. Singapore seemed to be in a state of recovery from what I had observed. Looking around the region at the time which appeared to be torn by divisive tendencies of various forms, be it political to social and economic inequalities of an explosive potential, The Lion City was starting to show signs of a robust recovery. The "rug" business was thriving at the time and the country saw a steady influx of foreign expatriates who were enjoying the opulent lifestyle of the wealthy, and were seen moving into some of the most expensive and trendiest neighbourhoods. Orchard Road was the mecca for shopping and you would notice visitors from all over the world, including the Malaysian Royal Family from the state of Johor, participating in late night retail therapy. There was also a noticeable climatic change in the corporate world, and expats with huge relocation allowances gave way to the emergence of a solid and sustainable retail industry. The "rug" business was nonetheless privy to this apparent growth. I settled in to my new position as a sales executive, and was in charge of data entry as well as providing support for many of the Company's prestigious projects at the time. Centre Point was a rather busy hub, and many of the stores would be open way past 10pm, and on some rare occasions, Robinsons' Store would be seen catering to the needs of the former Sultan of Brunei's consorts' shopping frenzy.

Days turned into a few months, and I was soon given my first overseas assignment. I can safely say that this experience went beyond the boundaries of normal propriety. As you read more into this magical journey I have enjoyed in this business, it may appear as a *cri-de-Coeur!* (Passionate outcry).However, to me, this was more about a conquest. This began when I was asked to fly to Brunei to furnish the Royal Family's Palace, undoubtedly the first of many memories of sheer opulence and wealth that I was privileged to have been exposed to. I said to myself, 'this job is starting to make sense"! No one in my immediate circle could say that they had been to the Royal Family's Palace in Brunei but here I was, a young twenty five year old lad, rubbing shoulders with the wealthy of unbelievable proportions. The trip was as memorable as I could have ever imagined it to be, and I returned to Singapore after spending a week in Brunei. The excitement was still lingering in the air but there was no time to rest on my laurels. It was quickly realized that my talents were being wasted doing data entry and providing sales support. Within six months of being on the job, another amazing opportunity was presented to me. Together with my mentor then, I was invited to work on the refurbishment and restoration of Singapore's quintessential landmark, The Raffles Hotel.

This was a mammoth project and we were asked to procure and deliver over seven hundred and fifty supreme and exquisite Persian Carpets which would be placed all throughout the hotel's interior and in the "all suite" guest-rooms. This sharpened my skills in project management and client relationship management. More importantly, I was thoroughly enjoying my work. Each carpet that I handled during this project highlighted a magical display of colour, design, language and depth, and in some unusual way, the appreciation of the art-form enabled me to focus on my mission and my quest, eliminating all feelings of apprehension that I had felt on my first day on the job. I excitingly related my experience to my family when I was allowed to make intermittent trips back home.

Any shadow of uncertainty that was hanging over the world economy seemed to be played out evenly as Singapore started to see more and more players entering the 'rug" market. Naturally, this resulted in an even playing field and buyers became more astute about their purchases and began looking for bargains. In the search for new ways to do business, and with the absence of social media and the internet, we had to resort to old fashioned marketing strategies and employed the direct selling approach. The first of many carpet auctions was born. This could be seen as a genuine tool to recognize the health of the carpet market at the time, as leading carpet companies would be seen engaging in weekend auctions that saw the sale of over one hundred carpets going off the auction block in one single sitting. This was an incredibly lucrative marketing exercise that saw the company's cash flow improve in leaps and bounds. Not bad for a days' work I thought and immediately jumped at the opportunity to try my hand at auctions.

My thirst for a new challenge in the business grew rapidly and I was known to be a strong and formidable contender within the market competition. The response I received was positively encouraging and mind blowing. I was able to create an ambitious, comprehensive and authoritative forum in which my audience were able to gauge very quickly on the best value rugs that they should purchase. It became a relentless affair from then on. Equally important to the success and growing authority of the auctions was the attendance of the senior members of the Hassan's clan, including the man himself, Mr. Hassan, who freely gave his time and valuable expertise in the first instance, and this created the much needed boost in my confidence. Subsequently, this also improved my relationship with the old man, who was not really known to be close to anyone.

Right about this time, I started to form a real affiliation for tribal rugs and this proved to be a very valuable source of inspiration towards my well-being later on in my life. The rugs in this category showed great subtlety in terms of the natural earth colours used and it gave me a sense of belonging, a sense of understanding the relationship between the people and their work, and the dimensions in which they functioned. This observation resulted in a better understanding of its popularity and importance in a market which was seen to be steadily gaining momentum year by year. The plateau of motifs and its relevant meanings also gave me a more astute sense of selecting the right rugs, not only for business but for my own personal collection as well. These rugs were part of history that were significant in all aspects of the study of hand knotted rugs and further enhanced the fact that just because a rug is at the cheaper end of the price spectrum, design and material quality need not be sacrificed. These rugs would speak to me in their own language.

As the months went by, my involvement in the business took on a more interesting role and I was promoted to the next level, and as the new assistant manager of sales. I was now in direct contact with the management and was given a more prominent position in key decision making activities. My "kingdom" was paying off its dividends. Then one morning, and rather unexpectedly, I was informed that I needed to move out of Imran's home and into another house which was a stones' throw from Centre Point. This was a pre-war house situated on the very much sought after address of Cairnhill Road. The houses on this street were all fully restored colonial villas and town houses and it was anyone's dream to be living on this street. I, on the other hand, was not welcoming this news with open arms. My enthusiasm level dwindled almost immediately because I was moving into the Company's warehouse.

The location was prestigious but the condition of the house was absolutely dilapidated, to say the least. There were three rooms upstairs which to me were completely inhospitable and I was shocked at the suggestion and decision to move me here. My house mate who shared the same house with me before was also made to move, but unlike me, he was already accustomed to the conditions in which we were about to endure. You see, he was from a remote village in Pakistan and any place in Singapore would have been heaven for him. The only consolation that came to mind was that the house reminded me of the old government bungalows that I had seen as a kid growing up in Malaysia.

The thought of moving here made me miserable and I was not impressed. After delivering so much value to the Company, I was expecting something much better than this. I was losing my "kingdom" and to make matters worse, I had been working relentlessly for almost six months without a break and I desperately needed a change in environment. While the journey to embark on this new mission in Singapore seemed to make perfect sense, and just when everything was falling into place, the anticipation of facing this new home was a catastrophe on a mammoth proportion. I felt as though my new home set the benchmark of compromising my desires of what a good and opulent life was all about. I kept reminding myself about my intentions and about the conquest which at that time, was at the centre of my universe. This uneventful move was seen as the onset of another new paradigm shift which I was not prepared for. While it set the tone in which I would drive myself at work and eventually pay a hefty price with my overall well-being, I decided that I had to push on and move ahead. Deep down, I knew that something didn't seem right. My dream of living the opulent life was vanishing from before my eyes!

I re-examined the sole purpose of embarking on this journey and I told myself that I needed to deal with this sudden and disruptive change in my unwelcoming environment positively. I knew that my immediate circle of friends thought that my reaction was a complete exaggeration but I was compromising, again, and this was not acceptable. It was disruptive and unnecessary. I found that

I was externalizing every single aspect of my life and the daily occurrences that I seem to be facing. It was time to intervene, I needed a self-initiated intervention. I turned to alcohol! What else was I supposed to do? This was a great escape for my altered state of mind and every night's escapades and charades would leave me completely plastered and with an obliterated ego. I felt like I was no longer living in a paradox since I had no real home – just like the nomadic weavers from the tribal plains of Southern Iran.

My immediate concerns began to disappear and the feeling of being invincible became the new force within me. I loved the night life and there was never a need to return home at night. I was known as the night owl and would retire to bed just before the sun would rise in the morning. My good friend Raj and the folks at Hassan's began to notice my change in behaviour, not to mention my reduced levels of concentration at work. I was gently reminded of my responsibilities and that any act of insubordination would not be tolerated. I was oblivious to what was happening at the time and my immediate circle of friends decided that enough was enough. I mingled with a small group of people whose penchant for hawker food and cold beer was second to none. This became my new night life routine instead of heading out to expensive bars and the trendy watering holes that I had seen on my first day in Singapore. This was a welcoming change of course and the dialogue which we exchanged made some positive inroads within my inner psyche. I was starting to recover from the miserable state of disarray that I had placed myself in.

For as long as I can recall, I have never been recklessly bold in defiance of convention. If I was showing any signs of audacity, it was always followed through with style and character. But now, I was behaving like a child whose toys have been taken away. Something had to change and I needed to break away from this routine habit and infuse a degree or element of sophistication in my quest to experience and do more other than to survive. As my boss at the time would say, think of it as character building and do something about it. I had big dreams of being at the helm of a company one day and I would often ask myself if I would be acting in this reckless way if I were a leader. I only knew what was going on around me the way it was projected within me. What was paramount to the idea of living within this self-inflicted state of misery was the paradox of priority. I was starting to justify my actions which deep down were not in my character. I realized that this was a choice which I had made and in order to change and experience euphoria which had been the initial 'modus operandi', I needed to stop externalizing my actions. This meant that it was absolutely imperative that I tap into my personal discourse which seemed to be prematurely clinging on to an idea of a pure energy state, and face up to reality.

My immediate environment was fine; there was nothing wrong with it. So what if my home was not a kingdom anymore, I ought to be thankful that I had a roof over my head. You see, I was still angry and unsatisfied because I wanted more. I wanted to expand infinitely with no compromises or conditions made. The thing is this was not being done right, and it today's language; this meant that I was not doing it holistically or spiritually. Therefore no matter how I tried to change, it was still a known fact that I was in an infancy stage of developing myself and kept competing. But who exactly was I in competition with? Evidently I was staging a war from within and unknowingly causing a massive tsunami of events to occur.

One of the most noticeable traits of my behaviour at the time was that I was always entangled in some kind of emotional web, and this was a web of deceit. I had to stop lying to myself and began reading on spirituality. I explored the concept of eternal life by Sai Baba and according to his teachings, we needed to choose an area of life, employ the instruments of our body and pursue happiness. This had to be real with no relevance to any form of attachment other than to oneself and the universe. However, at that time, my happiness was all about attachments to anything that seemed opulent and rich and it was mainly materialistic. There was nothing pure about it. I reminded myself of meeting the eldest brother at Hassan's who enjoyed his immediate surroundings by walking around either bare footed or in slippers. My desires were not measured in this way and success was measured in an unrealistic manner simply because of the competition that I had placed myself in. There was no way out and it was at this juncture that I started my search to allow my core human value to function. It never happened, not until very much later in this journey.

To make a change, I realized that I needed to realign my thought process in relatively small and acceptable doses. My first act of a conscious decision was to measure and map my journey. Let's pause for a moment here and realize something, I wasn't ill or in grave danger in anyway whatsoever. I was simply sulking from being deprived of a good life and as I have already stated rather eloquently, I despise failure or even admitting to the fact that I had failed. In this situation, I did not fail but I kept telling myself that I had. I was not progressing and my internal well-being was being battered by this sense of insecurity. I was not prepared to accept a lower standard of living simply because I had placed myself on a pedestal so high that falling off the ladder would amount to a psychopathic act of suicide. In my quest to map out my life's purpose, I needed to understand what inspired and made me "tick". I decided that my love for "rugs" would save my soul, my work would be my saviour and I was ready to redeem myself.

My family was not exactly the religious type, although they would frequent temples on Fridays, I often wondered if they knew what they were doing. Religion and spirituality would have been the obvious choice in my quest towards some level of self-redemption but since I knew very little about either one of the schools of thought, I needed another project to stay on course. I was adamant in my belief that religion was to play no part in my personal development. After creating this road map, I needed to chart my journey and actually sketched out my path on a large piece of paper, drawing out all the links and anticipating the blind spots – the impending catastrophic events that might occur. After all, it was a known fact that I was able to inflict these events onto myself rather effortlessly. I kept reminding myself that I needed to be honest and realistic about the path that lay ahead and its ingredients of well-being. This meant performing reality checks from time to time. Finally, I needed to continue pursuing happiness and this began with some serious soul searching. I can still remember to this day that I have often looked back and laughed at myself, commenting needlessly on some of the people who had been assertive throughout my pursuit. I know they meant well. Collaborating all these decisions also meant that I needed to have this charted map handy at all times and it was the first time in a long time that I began to prioritize some "me" time, that is to spend some solar time with myself.

There were no cell phones then, no emails to bother you and no tweeting or hash tagging anyone, no Facebook to comment to the ghosts on line or to poke or be poked online! All my experiences were real, with some human element involved. Taking some time off from the competitive and hostile environment that I had placed myself in was a brilliant act of bravery. I remembered what my colleague Raj had mentioned when we first met in Singapore, that taking a day off in this trade was unheard off. I needed to change this perception.

In the following months, it was paramount to my very existence that I make a list of what was important to me. I wrote rather unexpectedly in the following order: get married, buy a house, get a pay-rise and have children. There was no mention about living a healthy life or a prosperous life. I chuckled at the thought of getting married and memories of my grandmother and her arranged marriage activities made me laugh out more. Still, it was the thought that counts and I will love her to death for wanting only the best for me. After all the soul searching and what seemed to be a senseless waste of time, things started to fall back into place. I began to be more alert at work and started to dive back into my passion for rugs. My social life was also starting to improve and my friends and colleagues from work would plan twice weekly dinners and we'd end up in a nice place for after dinner drinks or even listen to a great band every so often. On one rather unexpected evening, my colleague Raj had called the office to say that he had arranged for me to meet some of his school friends for drinks and we would go with the flow. He arrived at my new and prestigious address in Cairnhill road around 8pm to pick me up and I noticed that there was a very attractive woman with him. I thought she was his girlfriend but was introduced to her who turned out to be his friend from high school.

I was immediately attracted to this new face in the front seat. That night, I was introduced to Rozana (Rose), who I referred to in the beginning of this book as my wife! Like I said *"In anticipation of a pending catastrophe, a tsunami of events might not exactly cripple you"*

5

Love and "sew forth"

"I tread myself fearlessly into a new territory of life, rich with solutions, woven intricately like a well sewn patch work – This is love"

Meeting Rose couldn't have come at a more opportune moment. I was entering a period of reflection in my life in Singapore and after what appeared to be an internalized tsunami of events, I needed to form a rotation that would have been best described as "turnkey" – a phrase used in the design world that initiates a change from inception to completion of a given space, complete with all the internal elements to forge a relationship between the space and its environment, not forgetting the occupants who would inevitably be living in it. My space was in desperate need of an overhaul and I was now on a self-renewed mission to motivate myself personally, not only as a means of surviving in the ever developing Lion City, but to a greater extent, a means of dealing with certain values that I had come to appreciate in life without losing a shred of my humanity. I turned to my love for my work and continued to surround myself with rugs.

Rose and I spent some time together talking and poking fun at each other on the first night that we had met and although I was a devil at that time, often seen in the company of women who seemed to gravitate towards me for some odd reason and vice versa, I wanted to know more about this woman who had made a huge impression on me. I was sure that gravity was dealing a favourable deck of cards here. Before we parted ways for the night, we exchanged contact details and I sort of knew that despite our immediate differences in our race and religion, I was about to enter into a new territory, completely unfamiliar to me but one that would prove to be invaluable on all frontiers. I knew for a split second that Rose and I had crafted a bond that would last for a while, but little did I realize then that through a series of events and occurrences, she would eventually become my soul mate, my partner in crime, my life partner, my wife.

One of the immediate concerns at the time was that having a relationship with Rose, being a Muslim, would be a battle for me in more ways than one, not out of prejudice for the religion or in her faith, but more of pleasing my mother and my family. You see, my life then was as if it was preordained. It was like a nicely woven rug with good colours, good detailing with an interesting tonal element. Well, that's what everyone thought! The perception that I would marry a Ceylonese girl seemed to fit perfectly into the notion of maintaining the family name. While there appeared to be some irregular behavioural traits being displayed by me, the overall idea that everyone had was that my decision in the end would end up pleasing the family, much like a rhythmic movement of an artist's brush stroke or a carpet weaver's hand. It was perceived that I would never do anything to tarnish the family name. However, I had other plans, and it would take almost a decade from hereon to realize this plan, but not without a series of battles, trials and tribulations, that eventually saw my entire family falling in love with this woman. The journey of love, intricacies and surprises unfolds....

After a period of six months of living in the Company warehouse, it was time to move as I couldn't take this environment anymore. Rose had visited me in this hostile space of mine and although she often kept her comments to herself, it was a known fact that she thought that I could do better. I needed to do something insanely different once again and not to mention audacious. My untrained eye had now come to accept certain attributes familiar to the human condition, my human condition and somehow there was this infusion of a personal branding experience, opulent and graceful on the onset and fearless in the appreciation of the endless variety of movements that characterized every aspect of my behaviour. I needed my own space, an apartment or a flat that would be mine. Although I was earning a respectable living at the time, renting an apartment would blow my budget to smithereens.

Now would be a good time as any to point out that I am, by no means, an expert in any particular field, but I do profess to being an ardent observer, and in this context, I strongly affirmed my allegiance to the fact that a change in environment was very much needed. It became painfully obvious that what I observed through my opulent experiences in a certain time and place, and what I consumed without knowing it at that time, certainly personified the virtues of a certain lifestyle that I had grown accustomed to. This familiarity within an acceptable level or standard of living which I needed to experience internally and externally was further elevated to another platform on the virtues of committing to a set of principles that I had lived my life by. I knew that despite the numerous times that I had fallen before, I was always able to pick myself up and stay firmly footed. With these values on life in mind, coupled with a sheer determination to remove myself from the horrible condition that I was living in at the time, I marched up to my employers and very calmly asked if they would be able to consider renting an apartment for me to live in. It was not the thing to do, but I felt that it was warranted, and that no one should be made to live under such deplorable conditions.

I don't think that the Hassan's family had any inclination of how bad a condition the Cairnhill Road warehouse really was in, but they definitely knew that no maintenance had been done to the place ever since they purchased the property for a whopping one million Singapore Dollars. This was an expensive piece of property and it was in a deplorable state. After some negotiating, the Company agreed to put me up in a HDB (Housing Development Board) flat in Ang Mo Kio, a local neighbourhood not too far away from the City and I was given an allowance of Singapore – currency $450 per month. This was in the early 1990's and rentals were fairly accessible if one were earning a fairly good income, although if you were a Singaporean, you would be encouraged to purchase a HDB property under the government's incentive scheme. I took this opportunity to look at numerous places and finally with the assistance from one of Rose's contacts, I managed to secure a three bedroom flat, fully furnished at a respectable Singapore – currency $700 per month. Since I was not going to starve with my contribution towards the rent, this was a great move and in a matter of days, I was liberated once again. Rose and some friends, including Raj, helped me move into my new flat.

Amidst the noise pollution from the main street and the noticeable amount of dust, I manoeuvred myself in this new neighbourhood with relative ease. In a matter of weeks, my brother and sister who were visiting from Australia had come over to stay, and it was also at that time that my good friend Marcia from Warrnambool decided to visit Singapore. I hadn't seen her since we parted ways after graduation back in 1988, so this was such a welcoming effort on everyone's part. I was a complete person again and naturally, after settling in, my mother and aunt visited, not once, but on many occasions. I was absolutely elated at the thought of having a home filled with familiar faces and a family to come home to. I even remember calling my mother once during one of my drinking sessions with my brother and sister and commented that all I needed now was a wife, to which we both laughed at emphatically.

By now, my state of mind was completely restored and I was like a raging bull, full of vigour and with a renewed sense of belonging. Everyone around me would attest to the fact that standing by my own thoughts and principles of a good life must be assessed without much recourse, and to worship the lifestyle that I had so cunningly and ferociously promoted and perpetuated would not be asking too much. Of course, how could I not recognize the fact that having any debate on this matter would be completely irrelevant unless it was to conjure baseless theories? In this case however, these theories were proving to be practical and justifiable.

Albert Einstein said that *"one should strive not to become a man of success but a man of value"*. Looking around me then, it was a period of self-realization, and as any young man of my age, I was indeed looking for some value in my life, but this did not mean that I was to become a man of value, certainly not at that time, but I was certainly becoming a man of character. One person who was definitely a man of value and character was my father. He was a teacher, educator, lecturer, mentor, husband, brother, an esteemed colleague to his work friends and a fantastic friend to many. His love for life and social interactions spoke volumes of his character and to me; he personified the concept of love in more ways than one. He loved his work, his family, and his sports and was basically a well-rounded guy. He had many friends and admirers and he was held very high on the pedestal of life. This was an insurmountable pedestal as far as I was concerned and I yearned to be like my father. I loved his demeanour and his zest for life, it was infectious.

Having distinguished myself as a seeker of the good life and having established a place that I could afford, I spoke at great length about my new home to my friends and family in Malaysia. They could not wait to visit me. In Singapore, this new space had become a resting place for many of my friends, including my special friend, who was now in my life on a regular basis, - Rose. I had identified the discomfort barometer that was plaguing my existence before this and I was able to establish a clear vision of the future. I needed to fit into that 'wet suit' and not feel choked. The program for change was taking its new course, and I was charting the coordinates on a new flight path of life, in a new and now more familiar territory, complete with a renewed sense of appreciating my environment and my humble abode. Needless to say, I took the opportunity to grace the floors of my new home with rugs, especially rugs made by nomads from the tents and cottages of Central Asia. Thy kingdom was born again and this time, King Dhushiyantha was in love.

In the introduction to this book, my brother Rajiv talked about my experience and mentioned about the 'existential infrastructure of life'. In this context, it would be appropriate for me to mention that this was, at the point of my having negotiated my new living environment, at its infancy stage. The foundation of decision making was being laid. The decision to make this move was the ultimate power that I needed. This enabled me to dive back into my work and my passion for rugs almost immediately. Rose would often remind me, even at the initial stages of our relationship that I should talk less and do more. So it was about this time that my first exposure in writing took its first bold step in the world of publishing. There was a publication called the financial planner and the editor Shoeb Kagda, a good friend and a rug enthusiast, invited me to contribute articles on the art of collecting rugs. One of the first articles that I wrote was about the weavings of rugs by the indigenous tribes and cottages of Iran and The Caucasus. I was insatiably connected to the wondering tribes and often thought about the investment value that was inherent in a certain 'pedigree' of rugs. I researched quite a bit on this subject matter and with the influence of prominent writes like Parviz Nemati, Jon Thompson and not forgetting Cecil Edwards, I summarized their work into this framework for further purview:-

"Before the late 19th Century, the design of Oriental Carpets and the peculiar style of each carpet weaving area reflected distinct cultural and historical influences which had remained uninterrupted for thousands of years. This remarkable legacy provided an enormous language of naturalistic motifs, all existing in balance and harmony. The weavers, who made these carpets learnt from early childhood, the grammar and vocabulary of their tribal and village traditions and with their mastery of weaving came the almost poetic ability to incorporate deeply held spiritual beliefs into the designs, be it traditional or otherwise. Although conservative, this long standing tradition gave the weavers freedom to improvise and compose their magical life story onto a carpet, or what we sometimes loosely refer to as a "rug". I have found that this interpretation of their language and sheer ingenuity, almost as if they were in a meditative equipoise, enabled

us to see their world in some sense of reality. They were able to paint a picture of a few million knots, often intertwined and complex into something simple, yet priceless. This is the art of the hand knotted carpet which remains the single most collectible piece of history to date"

Some of the carpets on display during one of my talks

This experience in writing stamped my "love" for my work and as time went by, my involvement in the business took on many roles, much to the relief of my personal well-being. I was now really enjoying my work and it all seemed to be sewn together into a patch of life which was artful and well received. Right about the time after I had spent almost two years in the business, and having entered into various dimensions of love and attachment, both in terms of my work and in my relationship with Rose, I began questioning my role as 'the' prominent male. I was hardly known to be egoistic but I loved antiquated phrases, dry sarcasm and I sometimes spoke in a manner that would 'piss people off'. Still, I was the seeker on all dimensions and while I saw myself as an intelligent man, I knew I was also prone to sulking and I amused and appalled my colleagues and bosses with many misadventures. This inevitably affected my manners and I was hardly able to counter tragic situations – I basically hated confrontation. I was, however, fond of over stating everything and exaggerated to a great deal and on one particular occasion, I distinguished myself in a particularly unpleasant way by dragging my colleagues on a wild goose chase. There was a particular client from Korea who had marched into our shop and asked to buy 1000 rugs for his outlet in Australia and he wanted me to head the store. All my memories of Australia started pouring in and I remember mentioning to Rose that it was my dream to migrate to Australia. Needless to say, she was not impressed but still allowed my ego to take its course on this relentless wild goose chase. I don't have to tell you how I 'crashed and burnt', only to affirm the fact that I never broached that subject ever again.

Not wanting to give up a good position in the company, I re-established my commitment to my mission at hand, and I threw myself at any task that came my way, often with a near fanatical and once in a lifetime zeal. Coupled with prodigious amounts of alcohol, anything seemed possible and I would push myself to the extreme. One positive outcome that resulted from my crazy antics was that I somehow developed an eye for detail. Thinking back, those days of happy delusional, spirited argument, grandiose dreams of the riches and opulently wealthy, I was just not satisfied with what I had, I wanted more. I would be seen getting involved in the business ostensibly, getting deeper and deeper into the weeds of every passing day, to the extent that I felt that I had the experience, vocabulary and a criminally astute mind. I was a danger to myself and to the people around me.

It seemed that my life up to this stage was predictable. I was a terribly emotional fellow and wanted some form of retribution.

The target that I had set for myself was shaping me but the fact remained that emotions would overpower my decision making process. And from what I had gathered according to some linguistic explanation, there are apparently six thousand words in the English Language that defines 'emotion'! Oh my god! I said to myself that I needed to go after my ultimate living standard and I was not prepared to be stuck in some emotional pattern. Going into this new adventure which seemed to be lit up with the colours of life restored my faith in the art of love and conquest. Meeting Rose and moving into my new home created a breakthrough and something sort of clicked and there was a moment of creation that resulted in the path of finding my next course of journey. It was time to look at life through a different filter and while I had already experienced my fair share of "drama", I needed to create some link between the emotional filters in my existence with the meaning of my life.

I realized now that the conditions of my life were not controlling my destiny, it was the decisions that controlled it. Much like in the context of writing this book, I woke up one day and decided that the title needed to be **"The Audacity of Survival"** and I was going to search the four corners of the world and the depth of my inner psyche to pen down the opulent experience that came with it. While the whole concept of love was still a pretty scary avenue to explore and embark on, I needed the love and I used the connection between the space that I had built, its relationship with the immediate environment, and the company of a gorgeous woman to create this assemblage in more ways than one. I restored some faith in intimacy, friendship and even a silent prayer to have these feeling close to my heart.

I didn't know what it was, but it sure felt like love.

6

Life in the fast lane

"I was tossed in all directions but I hung on and waited" – Awakening the euphoria in me

The jury was out and it was apparently adjudicated that my efforts were slowly but surely paying off. With my consciousness firmly affixed on the roller coaster ride that I had endured in the first two to three years in the professional world, the dividends were sweet as pudding, and completely in synch with my bank balance that seemed akin to the Persian Gabbeh rugs, with an intelligent arrangement of a subtle colour palette. For the first time in a long time, I actually had surplus funds and was feeling pretty excited about it. Tailor made shirts, Loake shoes and Pierre Cardin pants started to look good on me and I was the guy that would be seen shopping almost every weekend. Since it was also a known fact that I could easily be seduced into the lifestyle of the "successful", I needed to know how they functioned and what better way than to look to my right and left and I noticed my immediate superior actively making some serious money in the stock market. Needless to say, it didn't take much convincing and I dived right into the financial market.

If I knew then what I know now about the stock market and the tumultuous feeling of nausea caused by contra trading, this would not have been the 'modus operandi'! Still, it was something that I had to do, so stick around, and you will know how this new found activity created such a buzz in my life. This was 1994, and COE (Certificate of Entitlement) prices in Singapore had hit Singapore – currency $100,000 in the big car category. This meant that if you wanted to purchase a meagre Mercedes 190E, it would cost around Singapore – currency $290,000, give and take a couple of thousand. Imagine that, when a landed property in Malaysia would have set me back half of this amount, and don't forget, I would have gained a substantial amount on the currency exchange. I thought to myself: I will never be able to afford a car at this rate! This is when I started to see a glimpse of me being recklessly bold in defiance and it was 'audacity personified'.

Contra Trading was a big thing then, and one could trade on Malaysian Shares over the counter in Singapore. Now, this was by no means an indication that I had any knowledge on Malaysian companies, or even Singapore companies for that matter. I had zero knowledge on the financial market, and I was ready to risk losing as much as Singapore – currency $20,000 in one single week if the contra trade 'went south'. Locking in a price on a particular stock traded over the counter which was aptly given the name "CLOB", this should have already sounded all the alarm bells, but I boldly went ahead with my first trade of ten lots, that's 10,000 shares. The total exposure at the time was Singapore – currency $30,000. I did not have this amount of money at the time, but the stock was anticipated to go up by twenty percent in that week, and if I sold out within seven days, I could cash in the profits with no money down. I mean, come on, this was like Santa coming to visit you every day. So like a galloping black stallion, I did this, week in and week out, and after tabulating the losses versus the gains, I made about Singapore – currency $2000 - $3000 per month. This was equal to my salary then. Hobson's choice you say?

With a heightened state of awareness, I was beginning to look and speak confidently and this was reflected in my work. After spending almost three years in Centrepoint's Tabriz Carpets, I was ready to move to the head-quarters - Hassan's at Tanglin Shopping Centre. Here, innovation, literature and the true appreciation for the art form evolved under the tutelage of Suliman and Athar Hamid. Dhush Kuladeva became a household name in the rug business and I even emulated the behavioural traits of the Hassan's two brothers, who I might add, had a way of looking at customers. They would stand in their comfort zone; arms folded and emit a glare that could cut through ice.

Customers loved their arrogance and I was completely in love with this environment. I suppose the natural progression of things would have warranted some reward for all my hard work, but this did not seem to be forthcoming. In those days, and especially in a family business, an employee would not ask for a pay rise. One would wait patiently until it was their time. However, I was in a hurry to move on, and this was when I started to look at the list that I had made a couple of years back, and obtaining a pay rise was on the priority list. To get the attention of the bosses, I started to take on more responsibility and asked if I could head the "carpet appreciation classes". This was an informative session conducted over four weeks in which, participants would get to handle and feel the various categories of rugs and at the end of the course, they would receive a certificate of attendance, verified and acknowledged by the management and by me. How cool I thought! Suliman already knew my game plan and played along while Athar pretended that he had no inclination of what was transpiring. Remember what I said about this man when I first met him, he was not only successful, but a man of value.

The classes were introduced in grand style and I lectured on carpet appreciation to collectors, casual browsers and enthusiasts alike and this was exhilarating. I even remember my mother and my aunt, Mrs. Gana Jegadeva, wife of Uncle Jegadeva (my father's younger brother), attending some of my sessions. I was now teaching and also showing off my skills to two ardent teachers and English Language experts. As nerve racking as the experience was at the beginning, I began to really enjoy teaching. Naturally, with the advancement in my work and increasing revenue, I was rewarded with a handsome pay rise. This was sweet victory! The experience that I had gained from teaching proved to be precious not only at that time, but later on in life as well. I decided that the small three rooms flat in Ang Mo Kio was getting a little too cramped for my lifestyle, and decided to move to a larger apartment. I negotiated for an increase in my housing allowance on top of my pay rise but true to the colours of the Kashmiri clan, I did not get what I wanted. Still, it was better than nothing and I moved anyway, to Khatib, a neighbourhood further away from the city and from Ang Mo Kio.

Although Singapore's heartlands were already connected by the Mass Rapid Transit (MRT), this was still a good forty minutes journey to Orchard Road. Nevertheless, I wanted a larger unit and moved into a five room unfurnished flat. This place was huge; with a balcony large enough to have a ceiling mounted fan and a dining table in it. At this time, my mother's household furniture collection, her precious black cane sofa set and wooden dining table, complete with a rose-wood half- moon table and twin chairs, and brass side tables which she had lugged from place to place, needed a permanent home. I thought this would be the ideal arrangement and my mother was only too pleased to let me have the furniture. It was the perfect set up – beds, wardrobes, furniture, rugs, and oh! - A company car was thrown in on occasional days. Now I was starting to live it up I thought. In a matter of weeks, I was settled into my new apartment and when Rose came over to visit, she was shocked to see the size of the furniture, not to mention the odds and ends and of course, the rugs that were strewn all over the floor. This was thy kingdom, reinvented once again, on a much larger scale. Rose and I spent a lot of time in this place; we cooked and entertained our friends on a regular basis.

One of the perks of this amazing profession was that I was able to embark on overseas assignments and after travelling to Brunei and the occasional Thailand and Indonesian trips, the company decided to set up its first overseas outlet, in Bangkok. This was the roaring '90's, and Bangkok was definitely the place to be. I won't dwell too much into the night life in Bangkok at this moment for obvious reasons, but it must be said that one night in Bangkok was all you needed. I began to set the pace of life in the fast lane. I travelled to Bangkok, Jakarta and Malaysia on a monthly basis and took full advantage of stocking up the bar in my new flat from the duty free purchases. Moving in this new pace resonated well with my spirits and I acknowledged the fact that in order to take positive steps towards improving my life and maximise my passion in my work, productivity and purpose, I needed to reach a whole new level of physical and emotional well-being. Since I wasn't spiritual or could never grasp the concept of spirituality then, I conveniently left this out of the equation. I knew that my mind had a tremendous effect on my body functions and all I needed to do was to keep my focus levels in check. I would often exchange views on the wellbeing of human kind with my bosses through our various talks on life and religion when we travelled together.

At this particular moment in my life, I recognized one fact, that I was not healthy. Years of smoking and drinking were starting to take its toll on my health and I recalled one morning in Bangkok, when I noticed some bleeding from my bowel movements. I paid little attention to it at that time and attributed it to my lifestyle, spicy food, lack of sleep, excessive partying and late nights in Bangkok's side lane bars and strip joints. I kept telling myself that everything would be fine and looked forward to returning to Singapore for some much needed rest. My boss Suliman, who was known to be rather healthy for his age, would say that all the aspects of health are related and feed on each other. Even getting a feel of having all the parts work together will give us the experience of what a healthy life can really be. All this was just too profound for my liking. While we would enjoy the opulent spread of Asian delicacies at the Concorde Kuala Lumpur's breakfast buffet, he would be indulging in his cereal and yoghurt. What a crying shame I thought. Ironically, it was at that moment that I realized that "Life is what happens when you are busy making other plans" and I kind of knew what was in store for me, not in its entirety though.

Athar Hamid (my boss) was into Yoga in the early '90's, and I had read a little about meditation during my course of study in psychology. During one of our discussions over dinner, I asked if it's possible to observe the thought process objectively. I had read that an insight into meditation will reveal that if one were to withdraw the attention of the senses from the thought process, then it could be possible to observe it objectively. In today's context, this is referred to as the western philosophy on the study of the mind, but the eastern philosophy would contend very quickly that we spend too much time on our thought process. I'm still trying to grasp this contention. The study of the mind as I was exposed to in university was somewhat objective and not subjective. However, we did acknowledge that the science behind the study of the mind was real. In the eastern context, I have read that this goes beyond the mind. I wondered if I could use all this mind power to make money on the stock market!

Even in some remote state of spirituality, all I could think of was making money. It's no wonder that this subject matter evaded my thought process for a long time. However, one thing did cross my mind. If the oldest carpet ever made, which according to empirical data, was around the 5th to 6th century B.C., and it was recorded to have preceded the invention of writing, then what were the nomads and inhabitants of the cave period thinking of when they were crafting this magnificent art-form? If you were to look at the Pazyryk Carpet which is the name given to the oldest carpet in the world, it's 2500 year old ancestry brought about the emergence of a new level of appreciation in the area of the hand knotted carpet. My question is "could the weaver or weavers have been in a meditative state to have been able to craft such an incredibly fascinating carpet"? Surely this would have even influenced the invention of writing? An interesting point to note here is while I was researching some material to write about meditation, my sister lent me a book on the interpretation of the Baghavad Gita by Eknath Easwaran. In it, Easwaran writes

> *"I would not hesitate to call meditation one of the most important of human discoveries, an evolutionary development as important as speech or writing".*

It is my contention that the weavers of hand knotted carpets would have at some point, been able to transport, transcend and catapult their thought process into a pure meditative equipoise – much like euphoria. It was clear to me that I needed to write about this at great length and at some point in my life. I know today, that there are some mystics that are 'wired' all the time, and appear to be high on life. This apparently is due to their meditative state, not induced, but one that has been internally established as their way of life.

Back in Singapore, the work scope picked up tremendously and before long, I was at the helm of the advertising and promotions department and willingly endured the daunting task of being responsible for the profitability of my department. This meant that I had to report on the profit and loss of each month's revenue based on my input in the marketing of hand-knotted rugs. One area that enhanced the revenue aspect of the business was exhibition sales. I remembered my initial exposure in Australia when I had the opportunity to be part of the travelling sales team, and this embedded a deep desire in me to harness the end results of this event based business model. I started to organize events in Singapore and regionally and together with my exhibition team, we generated and maintained a steady track record. Malaysia was the first on the list and my cousin Anurendra Jegadeva (Anu), now a well-known artist, was starting his career as a feature writer for The Star Publications. Anu was instrumental in allocating some much needed media exposure for my events, and each exhibition which was held at the Shangri-La Kuala Lumpur received great reviews. I had my photo taken and was featured regularly in the papers and in The Times Magazine as an authority on carpets.

Our clientele of the prominently wealthy and politically connected grew exponentially, and it was not long after this period that the stock market was at its most appetizing period. My colleagues in Singapore were aching to get into a particular stock which was reported to be reaching its peak point. We waited for a short correction before going in for the kill. My brother at this time was graduating from The University of South Australia with a degree in Architecture and was working on his honours dissertation. It required him to travel to Europe, mainly Madrid and Barcelona, which were two known cities for its architectural splendours. This, of course needed to be funded and as the elder brother, I desperately wanted him to have this golden opportunity. He had saved up some money but it wasn't sufficient. I spoke to my broker about this particular deal and mentioned that I couldn't afford to lose, to which he replied, "don't do it". As stubborn as I was then, my colleagues and I decided to go ahead with the deal and we each traded a hundred lots, that's one hundred thousand shares with a Singapore – currency $150,000 exposure. It was nerve raking to say the least and as 'arse luck' would have it, the stock crashed by a significant percentage just one day after we went in. My heart sank to the bottom of the ocean and like the titanic and it stayed there for days. I remember the term "character building" that Athar Hamid used to impart on me and kept telling myself that the stock would turn around. By day five, we were down by an even Singapore – currency $20,000 each, and I was ready to pull the plug, when it started to gallop like The Black Night in The Melbourne Cup back in 1985. This stock did such a magnificent about turn that at the end of the seventh day, we all made a profit of Singapore – currency $30,000 each. And all this with no money down but with a lot of sleepless nights, and not to mention numerous fringes on carpets that were given instant haircuts!

I cannot begin to tell you how relieved and elated I was on this day and with the absence of mobile phones, I can still recall going into a phone booth in front of the Orchard Road MRT (Mass Rapid Transit) station and called up my brother in Australia and gave him the good news. Needless to say, he was positively over the moon and together with a group of his class mates, Rajiv went on to submit his dissertation after a well-travelled journey around Europe, and I am honoured and very proud to say that he secured a First Class honours in Architecture. Today, Rajiv Kuladeva is an architect, a project manager, design manager and an avid lover of his professional trade, and has been tremendously influential in the successful implementation of many of Kuala Lumpur's legendary landmark buildings and projects. I remember upon his graduation, and after a couple of years on the job after returning from Australia, he worked on the Kuala Lumpur Exhibition and Convention Centre, next to the KLCC (Kuala Lumpur City Centre) twin towers. I shudder to think what would have happened if that contra trade had gone south but in the end, it all worked out well. I was happy to have played a very small part in his journey then, with an immeasurable sense of euphoria!

My life in the fast lane kept getting more and more interesting. From the five room flat in Khatib, I made the next bold move by relocating into a new apartment in Tampines, which was another suburb in Singapore. You could say that I was one fellow who could not sit still. This time, I had a house mate, Ruben, who was seeing my sister then. Ruben had just joined Singapore Airlines and was a second officer, while I was quite settled in my profession as a "carpet wallah", so it seemed rather convenient that Tampines would be the preferred location, considering its proximity to the airport. Ruben and I moved in and the trade mark Punithavathy furniture collection went along, together with my collection of rugs. This flat was the base for all our respective family and extended family members to stay in when they visited. Ruben was not the type to cook and do house work, but he put in his fair share of cleaning the bathrooms and even helped to prepare our meals, which we ended up cooking on a regular affair. The interesting thing about this space was that we had a large enough kitchen to have two refrigerators, one for food and one strictly for beers. What a life! My sister was studying at the University of East London, and would naturally make our flat her base when she visited Singapore. Initially, the sleeping arrangement would be rather sorted in the sense that they would not share a room together in my presence since I was looked upon as the father figure for some reason. But as time went by, the dragging of mattresses in and out of Ruben's room in the middle of the night became a senseless act and the pair went about their affairs in an acceptable fashion. If the clan back home had known then, tongues would have been wagging like Rimba's tail, my sister's adorable four legged companion. It was amusing nonetheless. Copulation 101!!

With all the elements in my life seemingly set in motion, the overseas travelling received a much needed boost and I ended up on a plane almost on a weekly affair. The next exhibition venue was Indonesia and Jakarta was the main hub of activity. The Sari Pan Pacific would certainly attest to my presence back then in a way that my personal details were permanently in their booking system. On the same street was Hard Rock Café, and this became my regular haunt during my business trips. In Jakarta, I was fortunate to have met two very influential Indonesian families, both of whom had served under the Suharto regime and were tremendously powerful. I was often invited into their home and received great reviews from them on the work that we were doing in Jakarta. They spoke Dutch, English and Bahasa and it was never a boring moment when I needed to be in Jakarta on business. Having set the pace in Jakarta, the next venue was Bangkok. The generals who were in the government and the Than Pun Ying's who owned a string of hotels were seen as our regular guests and patrons of our most prized carpets. This was a trade that was receiving the much needed recognition and I was at the helm of it. I worked with great passion and enthusiasm and thoroughly engaged myself in this experience. The artistic explosion had taken on a new dimension in my world and the paradigm shift set the benchmark for the next phase of my life.

If I were to take you back a couple of years ago when I mentioned that just as I felt some sense of equilibrium in my life, I would have the innate tendency to 'screw it up' by examining its relevance, its positioning, its prevalence, and I treated good fortune as if it were a commodity that needed to be re-invented. I kept paying too much attention to my own thought process. To me, there was no such thing as "pot luck" and I could never be consistently happy. Complacency was a word that simply evaded my vocabulary, and I would detest anyone in my inner circle who would even remotely display any behavioural traits of complacency. I knew that life was ready to kick me in my "egg rolls" if I settled. I was looking for something else, a new experience perhaps, a mentor, a teacher but I was not looking for a religious or spiritual teacher. What I needed was some real down to earth guidance. At this time, just prior to the end of 1994, my boss and good friend Athar was into "Sufism" and was an avid reader of "life's revelations" by Khalil Gibran. The poet and philosopher was all he spoke off during that time. Athar or Hamid as he was known to me, was not the overtly religious type, although he was a god fearing Muslim and had never touched a drop of alcohol in his life. Hamid was also a lover of the night life and that's where we connected. My thirst for the good life started when I would spend countless hours with him and some of his "crony" friends from Malaysia, sitting in hotel lobbies drinking coffee and smoking cigarettes. Back then we could actually smoke freely in hotels unlike today, where smokers would be placed in a 2ft x 2ft yellow outlined box to 'air their lungs'.

Hamid introduced "Sufism" to me in a very light manner. If you were to look up the meaning of his name and see its relevance in Sufism, Athar was known as the Sufi Saint! Well, not this Athar, although many of his friends looked up to him as one. I think it was all related to his generous sized wallet, just quietly! Going back to Sufism, I was always afraid that it would relate to the Islamic teachings or faith and I simply wasn't ready to be a Muslim. However, I was assured that Sufism was all about the truth. That's it! I did some light reading and in writing this part of the book, I can safely and confidently summarize the subject matter as the selfless experiencing and actualization of the truth. Now, there is of course, some relevance in one's belief in Sufism to be the path leading to God. Since "god" was not clearly defined to me then, I accepted the opening line. Furthermore, the practice to go towards the truth involved love and devotion. This spiritual path in the Islamic faith is called "Tariqat" or the way towards god. I know, I did say that I was not going to go into this if it meant some resemblance or relevance to Islam but this time, the sheer simplicity, yet powerful message that was revealed in this search for the truth was just too good to resist. I had to know more.

Essentially, Sufism is a school for the actualization of divine ethics. It involved an enlightened inner being, not intellectual proof, revelation or witness, and certainly not logic. By divine ethics, we are referring to ethics that transcend mere social convention, a way of being. This apparently was the actualization of the attributes of God. Whose God I asked? You can probably figure out by now that my mind was in complete disarray, and it was clashing in every direction, and I was beginning to think that my quest for something more was beginning to feel like another futile effort. However, it was lingering in the air, and like when I read that very first passage in the Art of the Woven Legends about the significance of the hand knotted rug, I needed to decipher the message into smaller and more meaningful parts. I needed to know if anyone could be a Sufi.

Imagine this! I was told that whoever that comes into words is not Sufism. Sufism is nothingness and it simply means to become and not to hear about. Huh! What? Then how would one seek to experience the truth? It's about devotion as Hamid explained further, to become the perfected one. There was another approach which made a little more sense that is to go to the extreme first and then become. I knew that I needed to seek and find some answers but I never did. Perhaps I will, by the time I finish this book as the final chapter of my life. For now, I wanted an experience that personified the affairs of the heart, and maybe explore the psychology of spirituality. I have studied the psychology behind the spiritual experience before and it does involve the heart and the commanding self. The heart is considered to be the divine gift and it's often linked to a mirror which must be cleansed of the dust of the natural and material world until it becomes spotless, and reflects some element of the truth. If I did this, it would mean giving up all material possessions and I wasn't ready. And even if I managed to polish the surface of the heart, I would find ways to tarnish it. Hamid referred to the words of the Prophet Mohammad, peace be upon him, and said: "the heart is between the two fingers of the merciful"

The Commanding Self on the other hand is the face of power that divides man to satisfy all his instincts, be it animal, sexual to aggressive, it's the source of all man's bareness and impurity. I wanted euphoria to be the basis of my experience and asked if this could be the means to manifest the search for truth. This was when, and for the very first time in my life, I picked up the Holy Quran and was asked to recite a verse from it, in English. It read:-

*"Surely the soul of a man incises to evil, except in as
much as my lord has mercy (2:53). In order to return to
the truth, the commanding self must be transformed first
into the "blaming self" and then into the "self at rest".
The "blaming self" seeks perfection and reproaches
the "commanding self" for its passionate and animal
tendencies. The "self at rest" have found peace and
arrived at perfection."*

That night, Hamid and I spoke a great deal about Islam but he
never tried to convert me in anyway. He simply said that 'when
you're ready to find the truth', you'll know. God knows I'm still
trying to in all my forty two years of my life, he said. The next
day, we reconvened at the shop in Tanglin Shopping Centre and
I was getting ready to go on one of my trips. Hamid was not
really the affectionate one, but he showed his caring side when he
actually spoke. His friends would attest to the fact that he was not
one who was fond of talking in his early days, but now I suppose
he felt that he had a pupil, me, and he probably wanted to set me
straight. I never really asked him why he took that much interest
in me. Ironically, my father's superior in the teacher's training
college where he lectured before his demise, was rather close to
him, and he too carried the name Hamid!

Before I left for the airport, Hamid gave me a note which he had
written in his "buku lima" – the small notebook that we all used
to carry with us in our pockets which had the numbers '555'
written on the front. In it, we also knew that he had records of
all those who had borrowed money from him! I believe my name
was one of them. Anyway, the note read:-

*"The discipline and spiritual method of the "Tariqat"-
love and devotion, and the path to finding God will*

gradually purify your heart, bringing forth its spiritual qualities and at the same time transmute the "commanding self". When the Sufi attains a purified heart, he will also attain the "self at rest". It is in this regard that great Sufi's have said "Sufism is the abandonment of the self to the servitude and the attachment of the heart to the divine lordship".

At that moment, I realized that I was ready for a change in my life's purpose.

I boarded the flight for Jakarta that evening, wondering what was in store for me at the Wanandi Family Home in Cilandak.

7

The Unwanted Visitor

"I seek to live within the dimensions of comprehension only to explore mindless manifestations..."

At the home of one of Indonesia's most prominent business figures, I was invited to give a presentation on the distinguished weaving tradition amongst the Iranian Culture. This was a short and informative talk, with a fair amount of personal handling of old and antique rugs, since in those days, we hardly used power points or slides. My talks were more 'hands on', and I aimed to get the audience to participate by actually coming up either on stage or in a more engaging setting, to feel and touch a piece of history. This resulted in an immediate recognition towards the dazzling beauty and excellent quality of Persian Rugs amongst the small crowd. The night ended with some drinks and we parted with a strong sense of having achieved a breakthrough. You see, this business circle purchased a considerable number of rugs that night and I was left with a "high and buzz" which was quite unlike what I had experienced before, even more thrilling than my Brunei experience. I left with a huge sense of relief.

On the way to the hotel, the driver spoke incessantly about his employer and how powerful he was. Of course, I already knew who he was in the social and politically connected circle, and I had placed very high expectations on myself prior to embarking on this journey. All through the short flight from Singapore, I couldn't help but reflect on the conversation that I had with my boss, and I had to do well in order to impress him. I wanted my mission to be different, and this trip was particularly important to me since I was presenting such high calibre rugs on my own, unlike my previous engagements, when I would be accompanied by one or more of the senior entourage from the Company. Needless to say, the celebration that was forthcoming would be somewhat of a night of drinking and heavy partying. I gathered my things and went back to the hotel to have a bit of a rest. After a short nap, I was ready to 'hit the town', and where else, but The Hard Rock Café. The crowd had already gathered, and I had absolutely no idea where the people that I had planned to meet were. Under most circumstances, or in particular instances such as this, I would be completely at ease with the surrounding, and would mingle my way through the crowd. However, on this particular night, my predominant feeling was intense fear, and of a sort that I had never felt before. I attributed this sudden feeling of helplessness to fatigue and perhaps a heightened state of anxiety.

After shoving my way through the crowd, some appearing to be more amorous than others towards their partners, I found my group of friends. I casually mentioned my feeling at the time to one of them, but I don't think he heard me correctly, what with all the thumping and bashing of musical instruments in the background. It was on days like this that I would often be thinking of my achievements, and I would persistently be drawn to some sense of rationality while performing balancing acts with my emotional core. I was, nonetheless, ecstatically pleased with myself, and the party went into full swing, despite a lingering sense of uneasiness.

At about 4am in the morning, it was becoming instinctively obvious that we were all functioning on overdrive, and our consciousness was somewhat irrelevant at this point. Displaying no indifference towards anything or anyone around us, we were now the blatantly amorous bunch, much to the amusement of the other patrons in the club. Odd, but very aware of what was about to transpire, I made an about turn and decided that I had better get some sleep and sneaked out of the club. I would never have made it out alive if I had remotely mentioned my intentions to the troopers that I wanted to go back. Sneaking off was the best option, and I found my way back to The Sari Pan Pacific safe and sound! It was a short walk back, so there was no need for a taxi or the company of my driver. Although there were a couple of close calls that with one wrong move, I could have ended up in a brothel. Now, that would have been an interesting story to tell!!

Wrenching up my way to the room, my night of celebration was about to come to an end, and I was ready to 'hit the sack'. I would usually take a shower first before going to bed, but in my drunken stupor, I simply must have slumped into bed, fully clothed, with my shoes on as I recalled. On all my other nights out, no matter what condition I was in, sleep was something that came naturally and usually undisturbed. However, this night was an unusually disturbing one. I kept waking up with the feeling that someone or something was in my room! From the moment that I had dismantled my sudden fear the night before at the ridiculously crowded club, I was unperturbed, unfazed and behaved like the untouchables! Now, the fear was subconsciously conscious, and my conscience was telling me to wake up! I didn't immediately, but as the minutes turned to hours, I eventually decided to confront this bullshit that seemed to be messing with my mind, while others would either be fast asleep, while some would have had the most awesome experience of watching the sun rise! Well, it didn't happen in my room, that's for sure.

I was perplexed, 'pissed off', angry and had no idea what had just happened. This brought back memories of my school days when one of our neighbour's sons had accidentally stepped on a Chinese prayer altar, the ones that you would see on the road, or at intersections, often catching you off guard. The poor fellow was sick for days and he was even hospitalized in a mental ward. He had gone bonkers! Of course at that time, I thought all this was 'bloody baloney'!! But now, for some strange divine and satanic reason, I began to have my doubts, and my mind was racing in all directions. Let me tell you something, what I felt and sensed was not something that I had made up in my mind, if I wanted to have a wild imagination, I would have conjured up a story about a four way orgy, but this was insanely difficult for me to fathom. I pride myself on being a man of logic, and unless there is a clear indication that cause and effect has come into play, I would dismiss it. But not this time. I had to recognize the fact that I may have been spooked by some evil spirit or demon from another dimension. Here I go ahead, tempting fate! Well, since the sun was about to rise, I decided that there would be no point sleeping, so I showered and went downstairs to the lobby for breakfast. I was greeted with the customary "selamat siang pak" (good morning sir, in Indonesian) by the ever so chatty waitress, and she showed me to my table. The breakfast spread was simply delicious, the full works, and I had a very hearty meal.

I spent the morning catching up on the news and decided that I would do some shopping to take my mind of things before making my way to the airport. The shopping centres were not opened yet but there were a couple of small vendors who had already started their day early. I picked up some souvenirs and made my way to the hotel to pack and the driver was ready to take me to the Suekarno Hatta airport. The flight to Singapore was on time and I arrived in Tampines that evening in my new apartment completely 'shagged'. I unpacked my duty free goodies, had an early dinner and went to bed. That night was as peaceful as ever.

Back at the rug headquarters, there was a frenzy of excitement; I was carrying cash back from the sale that I had done in Jakarta. The 'top guns' were waiting and as I walked in, the first question they asked me was; "how was the partying last night?!" I paused for a moment and said that I had my hangover for breakfast! I got away with it naturally, as wonder boy was about to place a whopping Singapore – currency $275,000 in the hands of the bosses! What a moment that was, but true to the Kashmiri's, these moments of exhilaration usually fade away rather quickly when the chief says to you; "we're still $500,000 short for the month"! Go figure! One would think that they were buying up Cambodia! In any case, they day progressed quite productively and at around 7pm that evening, we parted ways and I headed home.

My sister was visiting for the holidays, and Ruben had just returned from a flight, so we took the opportunity to bond. It was drinking time again, and we headed out for the night and had a few laughs, while we "elbow lifted" in style – a phrase that I was accustomed to during my student days in Australia. That night, after settling into bed, I had another episode with my unwanted visitor. I'm usually the sort of person who would live by abiding to some degree of comprehension, but now, it seemed that I was beginning to entertain this unwanted visitor. I began to question my destiny at this point and wondered if I was paying for all my past sins. Now, hear me out on this story.

According to my sister, I was having a rather consummate conversation with this visitor and plates were flying all over the place. How did I get to where the plates were, obviously the kitchen, and then to my bedroom without knowing it? Ruben had apparently walked into my bedroom and saw me literally conversing with this "thing"! Who was it? What was this thing? I was, nonetheless totally consumed by this episode, and displayed absolutely no sense of awareness of what I was doing at the time, and in the morning, there was absolutely no recollection of what had transpired the night before, until very much later, when everything would slowly surface to reality. My thoughts were not aligned and the emotional state that I was in was definitely cruising vertically and horizontally. What I do recall very clearly is that this unwanted visitor would suffocate me in my sleep, and almost prevent me from moving. I sometimes felt like there was an elephant sitting on my chest. I could not breathe and wanted to rip my chest open to see what the hell was in there. I sat and pondered upon this second episode that had somewhat gripped my sense of imagination. I began to talk to some people, and at the time, they were faith healers who immediately said that I was possessed by the "demons" of the after-world – spirits. Oh! Come on! This can't be right, these things don't exist, I said. I surely had my doubts at the time I uttered those very words, but I was applying some degree of logic here, and as a man whose faith in the living planet was about logical thinking and not some ghost like nonsense, I was really having a great amount of difficulty dealing with this "crap"!!

As I mentioned earlier, when these types of occurrences start to plague my life, I would question my destiny and in this context,

I knew that this had to be determined on an action plan. I had to bank on a strong mind set, while recognizing that this shift in my thought process would not guarantee some reasonable explanation to what had transpired. It had to be looked into in order to preserve the sanity of my well-being, and in a very small but significant way, ask for some divine intervention. Yes, I was looking to GOD for some grace. I kept telling myself that if I did the right thing, perhaps change my lifestyle, stop drinking and all that excessive partying, maybe the higher power would 'cut me some slack'! Another mindless manifestation perhaps! I had no idea where this was heading but it was time to make a bold decision rather than to simply wait and see what would happen. I talked to my immediate superiors, to Rose, to my sister and Ruben, all of whom had different approaches to understanding this dilemma. For my sister and Ruben, this was perhaps amusing as well as worrying, watching me dwindle emotionally while maintaining some confidence – plus it also gave them the opportunity to keep an eye on me. On the other hand, I knew that if I consulted someone who had dealt with this type of interference before, they would help me change this force that seemed to be controlling me and the conditions of my life.

I resorted to seeing a medium, a "bomoh", a faith healer and a spiritual healer who had some mystical power to heal the soul and send this rude visitor away for good. Believe me when I say that this was probably one of the most difficult decisions that I ever had to make simply because this went against everything that I believed in."

> **"I seek to live within the dimensions of comprehension only to explore mindless manifestations…"**

This is me, in my entirety, and now, there was an apparent shift in paradigm. But since I was acting like a bloody lunatic, especially at night and in my sleep, or prior to falling asleep, and waking up the entire household, ranting and raving, I needed to change my emotional wire. There was no other apparent alternative, not at that time anyway. I recognized that the mind at that moment was not in synch with any sense of reasonable discourse, and I was in danger of making disastrous decisions, one that would inevitably affect my personal and professional life. I was a rising star in the company and in the industry, and I had worked very hard to get to where I was and I was not about to let some unrelated force consume my life. It was quickly pointed out to me that someone in my circle wanted to hurt me, to hurt my sheer existence and send me back to the dark ages – this person wanted me dead.

It could be said that some people in my inner circle were utterly envious of my career advancements and the opportunities that I had been receiving from my bosses. I was the last member to have been included in the Hassan's clan, but I rose very quickly to the top, almost second in line to a top management position. This did not sit well with some forces that were beckoning my general well-being. Perhaps I was sending some signals to indicate that I had become rather arrogant with my success, or that I was willing to invite any kind of trouble since I displayed some invincible behavioural traits. This was my personal "blue print" so to speak, and it affected my state of mind all the time. I would draw on past experiences and recognized the symphony or the tune between what I desired most versus what I feared most. I desired success and I feared and despised failure. This was not a difficult concept to grasp, but I was increasingly aware that what I desired and what I yearned for were not necessarily in synch.

The "Bomoh" (spiritual leader in the Malay Language) mentioned that the only way to deal with this type of trouble was to identify the source, as in the person behind this, and send a message back to them. WHAT!!? This was completely unacceptable to me. All throughout my life, I had, up to that point, lived by certain sets of rules and principles, although, I was known to have broken these rules every now and then. There was never any harm done though. Now, there was this sudden turmoil of something that was non-existent, and it was becoming contagious, and in all this outer world calamity, my condition, my well-being, and my emotional wheel was further being internalized by this feeling of rage, anger and fear. Underlying all this confusion was the fact that I was about to embark on some voodoo nonsense and this was the apparent solution to my prevailing dilemma. I kept clashing with this approach. I was beginning to really envision a clear division between myself internally while realizing the urgent need to overcome this problem and I needed to make it go away.

Scores of people with various approaches, some of whom were drawing from personal experiences, were telling me that I needed to do something urgently. I had to be relentless in this pursuit, but I was stuck in the twilight of conflicting views. I told my friends and the "bomoh" that I needed some time to digest this but they kept the pressure on, even to the extent of providing me with a horoscope of what my life would be like if I were left crippled by this insane act of "black magic". There, I've said it. There it is, in black and white, it was indeed black magic, and to my rational self, this was insanity of the highest form.

By now, the episodes of this unwanted force disrupting my daily routine started to take on another dimension. It would follow me wherever I went, even on my overseas trips. This meant that no matter where I slept, it would be ready to disrupt my night totally, and in a spirited fashion. Oh My God! Who have I 'pissed off' so badly that they had to resort to this? Now I was scared, petrified and really worried that I might not even make it back home when I went on my weekly business trips. This damn thing was out to get me and I finally realized that I needed to be part of this larger issue which had created layers and layers of uncertainty in my inner psyche, and to a large extent, my disposition. This was the beginning of a new chapter in my life for I can now tell you that this went on for many years, well into the twenty first century. We will re-visit this insane force again in my journey, perhaps realizing that this force could have been a woman, who was obsessed with me!!! Rozana, you need to save me now, I said to myself!! I needed to stop this stupid riddle from haunting me.

One thing was for certain. I looked back at my life's track record, my personal blue print, which I had mentioned earlier, and realized that in living by those principles which I started to identify very early in life, to completely and totally chase after success, somewhere along the way, I started to go off course and went against it. I went against those rules and principles. This abrupt change in momentum caused a major collision and inevitably resulted in an increased state of stress! The atoms in my personal discourse in life had collided with each other and the stress that followed became a magnanimous force to deal with. I was not receiving the guidance that I needed and I was not in favour of the "bomoh's" approach, so nothing was really done to manage the crisis that I had encountered from the presence of my unwanted visitor. I did realize however, that the stress that I endured was not because of all the conditions that were prevailing at that time, but it was attributed more to the meanings and significance that were given to those conditions. As such, I decided to ignore this crazy visitor and carry on with my life.

This was initially seducing my judgement, and made me do stupid things. I was entertaining its presence and it had no stop. What I needed was progress, I needed to make a change and it needed to be done urgently. A breakthrough was about to happen.

I looked at this episode of my life as a tiny little crisis, although blown up in proportion to a significant level at times, this was still a crisis, and when things like this happen, there's no subtle way to remind us that we need to change. It melts us down and asks us to re-examine our life, to create the reinforcements that we need to progress to the next phase of life. Perhaps it was time for me to change my behaviour at work, to be more open and understanding to my colleagues, to show some empathy and to stop resting on my laurels. I had work to do; my mission was far from complete. In the end, my sister reminded me that it was because of my crazy lunatic behaviour that the mattresses stopped moving and it became a permanent feature in Ruben's bedroom! How convenient!

8

Expanding the moment

"In this moment of an open ended level of consciousness, I sensed the inevitable" – Family history revisited

One of the observations that I experienced while dealing in rugs was how the incredible art-form had matured over the "passage of time". The notion that these hand crafted gems would simply appreciate aesthetically the more it was used, revealed a whole new world in appreciating this phenomenon. With the passage of time, my personal involvement in the business grew exponentially, and I was steadily climbing up the corporate ladder. You would probably recall that the old man Hassan was not exactly the sociable type and I craved for his attention, much more than anyone else in the establishment. As time went by, our bond grew and we started to converse more, I could feel that he was taking some interest in my contribution to the business.

The old man was a cricket fanatic and since I played this sport during my school days, and later on in university, this game was the mutual link that brought us together, much like how it forged a bond between my father and me. If memory serves me right, he would describe the game to the curious few by a simple statement, "when you're in, you're not really in, you're out". "When you're out, you're not really out, you're in"!! Fascinating! We loved the thrill and would either watch the matches on television or listen ardently to the commentators on the radio. This was 1994 – 1995, and I soon found my common interest in cricket opening up "doors" for us to forge an unusually close bond.

Old man Hassan was also a gin rummy card player and he would partake in long overnight rummy sessions with his brother in Kuala Lumpur. On any given day, we would, at a moment's notice, jump at the chance of taking a drive to Kuala Lumpur, just so he could meet up with his brother, while I would use that opportunity to see my family as well as bond with some friends. I'd go bar hopping after dropping off the old man in his brother's house. All throughout our journey, he would apply me with his early trading days of going door to door, selling carpets to the rich and wealthy rubber estate managers, who lived in huge palatial government provided bungalows. I thought to myself, what a veteran! He personified all the class and humility of a rich and well-travelled 'carpet wallah'. I wanted to be like him, but with a few short cuts here and there. You wouldn't catch me knocking on anyone's door trying to introduce rugs, much less to a wealthy landlord or a smug estate manager. My stammering would have sorted it out!! Still, I had the Toyota Camry to myself, and would roam the streets of Kuala Lumpur with my brother, who by then, had returned to Malaysia and was employed with an Australian architectural firm. Rajiv rented a nice semi-detached double storey house and my mother decided to move in with him. So once again, we had our family unit intact and my sister too, would visit during her term holidays. Priya had, by then, left Australia and was now studying in The United Kingdom, pursuing her passion for social work and working with the underprivileged.

This was a time of great family gatherings for us all, and needless to say, when the old man would express his wish to go to Kuala Lumpur, I was the fortunate one to accompany him.

Right about the same time, Ruben, who was then my house mate, and I, decided that living in Singapore was getting expensive and we wanted the experience of living on a landed property, with a sprawling garden and maybe even enjoy the company of a dog. I was comfortable in my position in the company, and Ruben was already ascending the ranks in Singapore Airlines as a pilot, so we thought that the best option would be to move to Johor Bahru, a stone's throw across the causeway from Singapore. We thought that we would be able to save some money while living comfortably in a nice house and after looking around at a few estates, we settled for Kempas, an already developed residential estate in the suburbs of Johor Bahru. Since I was going to be commuting on a daily basis, I negotiated a deal with the company and was granted the use of the company car. This was a well-deserved break because I was initially commuting by bus, and this was not very appealing. You could not imagine me, the spoilt brat, lining up every morning, getting all close and personal with the regular commuters, to take what often seemed like an eternal bus journey to Singapore, not to mention putting up with some commuters who would not have taken their morning shower. Unintimidated as only the arrogant can be, I would start to voice out my disgust much like honouring the odour from someone who had just come off the late shift from the local abattoir! Yes indeed, I made it known that they stank to 'kingdom come'! The strong and offensive smell emitting from my fellow commuters was just too much to endure. So the company car was a breath of relief and the daily commute ended up being an effortless affair.

Life was good; I had a great job and had nothing to complain about really! Towards the end of 1994 and early 1995, my sister Priya decided to wrap up her studies and returned to Malaysia. Since her relationship with Ruben was already moving towards an eventual marriage, we talked about it, and it was decided that she would stay with us, while pursuing a career in Singapore. Priya didn't take long to settle in and was successful in gaining admission to a local neighbourhood school in Singapore as a student counsellor. This was a big break for her and with this pretty much sorted, our life as a family unit was once again, complete. The natural progression of events then saw my mother move in with us and we even had "Chivas" my brother's German Shepard sent over from Kuala Lumpur, since he was about to move into an apartment after my mother left his rented house. With the family unit taking shape, we settled into our new home and would appear to be enjoying our daily dialogue of magnificent home cooked food, not forgetting our twice weekly visits to the local Chinese restaurant for a change in palette!

You would probably have figured out by now that I am a creature of habit and by society around me. My external world meant a great deal, and I thrived upon other people's perception of me. I had also come to value the preciousness of time after being in the professional world for about six years since graduating from university. The melancholic reflections of my life thus far only indicated that time existed as part of the imagination of experience and this proved to be helpful in my life because I viewed time in my life as a telling prism, through which the emotions, meanings and values of my life could be perceived. I even started to notice how my life up to the moment, followed lines set by society, and I was beginning to find it difficult to keep promises that I had made to myself. I began to question the whole element of time spent versus time invested and it was casting a huge doubt within my inner psyche that I was not achieving what I had set out to do, simply because I was not having fun.

I was working like a well-oiled clock, with its pendulum swinging in motion, but there seemed to be something missing. I couldn't put my finger on it then, but what was clearly apparent was that I was beginning to lose weight. I knew that I had been spending my time in a relentless fashion towards achieving an acceptable level of success, but it was not serving me in a much needed humane way. What became more dangerous and critically obvious was that I was starting to detach myself from the notion of time that I had come to value and treasure. My relationship with my time and time around me was beginning to lose its enchantment, and I was measuring its relevance as a mental block of quantifying actions which was clearly lacking in depth and meaning. There was no "soul" left in what I was doing. I needed medical help but this was not my immediate reaction to the situation.

At the office, my colleagues and bosses started to notice my lack of energy and asked if I was having any problems, family, personal or otherwise. I told them that I was probably just tired from all the running around and constant overseas travelling, and that this was a sign for me to slow down. My inner voice was telling me to stop this insane overloading of my life with crazy activities, but who listens to inner voices when logic dictates? I was doing well and had already created a solid footing within the business community, and I didn't see the need in slowing down. So, I sought the help of a Chinese medicine man whose "magic" cured me temporarily. I went ahead with my life's purpose.

I realized with greater understanding that time had changed me, and I don't mean only the passage of time. Up to the moment, I had already invested six years of my post-graduation life in the business world and was not about to give in to the slightest bout of pain and discomfort. Looking around me then, I could sense that time was like everyone's silent enemy, the force that would either break or make someone. People around me talked about wasting time, killing time, passing time and some even doing time, and I refused to allow myself to be caught up in a moment of silence or idleness. That would have made me crazy, so I decided that I would seek some alternative treatment for the pain, which by now was consuming my lower spinal area. I had ferocious back aches and this resulted in my visiting my Chinese Sinseh at least three times a week. He used "*chi*" – energy that he would transmit from his palms on to my body without even touching me. I could feel the heat he was emitting on my back and oddly enough, these types of treatment made me urinate almost immediately, sometimes even losing control of my bladder.

Embarrassing to say the least, I pushed on with the treatment and continued the assault on my body, travelling almost eight to ten times in a month to Indonesia and Bangkok for work. At about this time, I would often reflect on my father's relatively short life, who left us one month short of his 50th birthday, and I had come to adopt the strategy that since life was pretty much a mortal event, there was only so much time for me. Even though I was not in any danger of any kind, neither was I suffering from an incurable disease or illness, I adopted the strategy that living life to the fullest meant cramming in as much activity as I could, and take on each day's challenge as a daily course of vitamins. We all remember October 19th, 1987, when the world spun into an economic turmoil from the disastrous crash on the world financial market. This type of uncertainty reminded me that everything around me needed to function within a time frame and I needed to set goals and limits to rake in as much as I possibly could, irrespective of what damage it was doing to my health and spiritual wellbeing.

This was now late 1995 and although I was seen to be doing more to achieve more, something didn't sit right with me, and I began to have all those feelings of emptiness and dissatisfaction all over again. I mean, what the hell, I had just gotten over one bout of pain and I thought that I had dealt with it, and I was able to function at full speed, but somehow I felt that I was achieving less. I had this nagging feeling that I was missing the plot so to speak, and I decided that enough was enough. It was time to get proper medical assistance, and after consulting my brother in Kuala Lumpur and some of my cousins who were already in the medical fraternity, I went to The University Hospital in Kuala Lumpur to get an M.R.I (magnetic resonance imaging) done on my lower spine. When I arrived in Malaysia, everyone was shocked to see how much weight I had lost, but I still thought nothing of it. Deep down, I must admit that my thoughts at the time revolved around the notion that I was probably dying of some disease that could not be explained. Still, I put on a brave front and did the test, only to find out that I had a slip disc in the lower back (L4, L5 and S1) region of the spine. This was treatable and all I needed was some bed rest and the doctors put me on a pain medication.

This was Tramadol, a tablet according to the journal of medicine, consisting of a "centrally-acting atypical opioid analgesic" with additional *"serotonin-norepinephrine-reuptake"* (antidepressant drugs) with inhibiting effects that was used to treat moderate to moderately severe pain. I was not very happy with this mode of treatment, but it was a better option than surgery, and I was never going to sanction any type of surgery on my spine. With a strict bed rest regime which lasted for almost a month, and almost going crazy as a result of not working for that period, I returned to work, rejuvenated and recharged, all ready to take on my tasks and responsibilities. At that very moment, I realized that instead of trying to speed up my life, I needed to make some time to slow down, to drop in, and to notice things, to really settle in my life and pay attention from moment to moment, instead of charging like a raging bull. You'd think that this experience, which I must add, was the first medical intervention that I had endured in my thirty two years of living, apart from an appendicitis surgery at the age of nine, would have woken up the instinctive side in me, much like the one that I had experienced on the day that I saw my father take his last breath. However, it did nothing concrete apart from creating a sense of awareness that life had no guarantees, that anything can happen, and we needed to be prepared at all times. So with the passage of time, I persevered and urged myself to push ahead.

The year was coming to an end and 1996 was around the corner. I would usually pick up some books of inspiration at the start of each year, perhaps as a reminder that as a seeker, I was still in search for the ultimate living standard, and I admitted to myself that I needed all the help that I could get my hands on. Combing through the bookshelves at one of my favourite book haunts in Singapore, I came across a book by Lou Pritchett who authored "Stop Paddling and Start Rocking the Boat". This was a book about accelerated change and in his book, Pritchett talked about why we all need to rock the boat. The synopsis of this publication was enough for me to realize that I needed this nudge in the right direction. In particular, one contributor wrote:-

> "*Thirty minutes with Lou, and you are ready to go out and slay dragons, reorganize companies, and completely*

*redefine the idea of working with customers. That's
Lou Pritchett…. Lou is pointing the way to the future,
to relationships that go beyond solving problems with
products and services that result in businesses coming
together in more meaningful ways"*

This was exactly what I needed. You see back then, work was my number one priority, followed by family life, doing mundane things, reorganizing my social life and spending time with myself. My work defined me, it personified my mission in life, and it reinstated the whole concept of that opulent lifestyle that I was so desperately trying to achieve and maintain indefinitely. I didn't know then that this was not a realistic world within the sphere of normal comprehension. I only knew what my heart revealed and my heart was racing at full speed, sometimes skipping a beat, just to finish first in every race. What I did not realize is that whatever I was doing, it was always *to* something or someone, instead of *with* something or someone. This would have surely assisted my endeavour to achieve anything that I wanted, to expand the moment in which, an open ended level of consciousness would exist. Instead, it created another demon, an illness that was apparently part of my genetic lineage and one that I had no inclination towards.

This brought about a visit to the doctors that eventually sealed my fate that I had welcomed a family history which had apparently prevailed for more than three generations! The story begins in one particular morning, as I was ready to leave my home in Johor Bahru for work. I remember this day clearly, because I didn't have the car with me, but since I was already quite comfortable to hail a taxi directly to Singapore, I thought nothing about the trip or felt any inconvenience in the journey ahead. My mother had cooked a scrumptious breakfast and I said my good-byes and made my way to the Johor – Singapore taxi terminal. As I left the house in Kempas, I felt a strange feeling inside me that something was not right and a voice was calling out begging for a reply.

As arrogant as I was to people around me, I was also the nonchalant type, and often dismissed anything that I would place little emphasis on. I naturally ignored the signs, blaming my recent bout of pain and discomfort on incessant fatigue, coupled with the fact that I had been sitting on my arse for a whole month, so I naturally attributed this to exhaustion and pushed on with the journey. As I was about to arrive at the terminus, I felt a very sharp pain in my groin area and lower abdomen and it was like a knife piercing me repeatedly, so much so that I vomited in the taxi, much to the disgust of the taxi driver. Nevertheless, he was sympathetic and probably realized that I was in no condition to get out and hail another taxi so he very kindly drove me home. I decided not to go in to work, quite unlike anything that I had ever done before. Work was my life, and I loved what I did for a living. On the way home, I started to reflect on a month before this day when I was interviewed by CNBC Asia and Asia Business News on investing in carpets and I was already a foremost authority on this subject matter. This force that was soon resonating throughout the carpet world gave me a celebrity type status, with the well-heeled and discerning carpet collectors. Now, I was helpless, I was clueless as to what was going on and I was no doubt, in excruciating pain.

I knew that I was in trouble and this time, it seemed serious, simply because I was about to skip work - this was simply not done, not in my world that is! A couple of months back, I was in Kuala Lumpur, where I was diagnosed with a slip disc and at that time, despite the apparent weight loss, no one had pieced the symptoms and prognosis together. However on that very day, having decided not to go in to work, this was an experience of deep seated anticipation and agony into the remote possibility that I was gravely ill. Upon arriving home, my mother was shocked to see me back, and she was even more worried that I was crouching in pain, barely able to walk, and as I made my way to the front door, I apparently slumped to the floor and was not able to move. No one else was at home, my sister and Ruben had already left for work, and mum was left with the daunting task of attending to my almost dead weight.

Mum called my office and spoke to the elder Hassan and mentioned that I would not be going in. The company acknowledged the call and mentioned that I should just rest. However, I was not known to sit still and do nothing, I was fond of reading but only during bedtime, all my other activities were usually work or socially related. If I was not working, I would be seen in the pubs, any pub, as long as the beer was cold! Well, it was clear as day that I needed to rest and get medical help. As stubborn as I was, and I attributed this to my maternal side of the family, and decided to stay home and did absolutely nothing but eat, watch television and slept like a prince! After a couple of days rest, I resumed work and was all geared up again.

Back at the rug head-quarters, the Hassan's family was attentive to the fact that I had been falling ill a little too often, and suggested that I seek medical attention by undergoing a full medical examination. I hated hospitals, doctors, nurses, needles, gowns, wheelchairs, and the smell of antiseptic that would make a skunk throw up! But there was apparently something transpiring deep within the walls of my bladder and I had no idea what it was. My Chinese Sinseh friend examined me again and this time, he mentioned that the source of my back pain was originating from my bladder and abdomen. Then, through some unusual stroke of bad luck perhaps, I noticed a patch in front of my trousers when he was treating me with his "Chi" method and it turned out to be bright red blood – I was urinating blood. "Holy shit, mother of god, I was petrified". Blood in the urine! How is this possible? I was so naïve to the conditions that were often prevailing with anyone who had a urinary tract infection. This was apparently the result of a cyst in the bladder, or cystitis in medical terms.

The "Oh shit" feeling consumed me and I was still unable to place the pieces of the puzzle together - weight loss, and blood in the urine. The underlying theory was that I probably had some infection that needed immediate antibiotics treatment. Suliman, the eldest of the Hassan's brothers mentioned about a procedure done in a clinic where the specialist would scan my bladder to see if there was anything abnormal. I agreed to get this done at The Mount Elizabeth Hospital in Singapore and since I was covered by insurance, I wouldn't need to chop off my arm to pay for the procedure. The scan was done to rule out the possibility of a premature growth, benign or otherwise. The results came back and I was apparently clear of any form of abnormality and I cannot begin to tell you how relieved I was, even though I had ignored previous signs of something not being right. I looked back about a year prior to this episode and recalled on a number of occasions that I experienced severe burning sensations during urination, and this also led to lower back pain. However, now that the results were negative, and that I was clear of the possibility of having an infection of any kind. I felt confident that this was just a temporary episode and with a little bit of care and proper maintenance, things would get back to normal.

Months went by and all seemed well, until one uneventful day, when my world literally collapsed. The pain had taken on a new dimension; it was crippling to say the least. Up to this point, I knew deep down in my soul that I had a problem, but as an individual who lived by some logical sense of thinking, my thought process revealed one simple fact. I needed to accept a certain measure of responsibility for my own destiny and now it seemed destined that I was heading downhill as far as my health was concerned. The notion of taking responsibility was not new and the general philosophy was that one should adhere to a self-realizing prophecy when something didn't seem right. Norman Cousins wrote in his "anatomy of an illness" that ancient physicians were so familiar with the natural power of the organism to control disease that they invented for it the beautiful expression, **"*vis medicatrix naturae*"**, "the healing power of nature".

Norman Cousins identifies the natural recuperative mechanisms of the body with the processes called homeostatic responses, namely, the natural processes that enable the organism to return to the "normal" state in which it was before being disturbed by a noxious influence. In my case, I had no idea what had disrupted my well-being in this sudden manner, and despite a last minute intervention of some homeopathic treatment, my condition was getting from bad to critical. I needed urgent medical intervention and without wasting any more time, my late uncle Dr Mahadeva, my father's youngest brother, had called one of his contemporaries in Johor Bahru's Puteri Specialist Hospital to get me admitted and I was attended to by a Dr. Shanmugam, a general surgeon, who had dealt with cases like mine before. Before the admission, I was rolling in pain in the waiting room and a lady who was sitting next to us signalled to my mother that she should alert the nurses and perhaps I would be allowed to jump the queue. Whoever she was, I hailed this woman as my guardian angel because I would have been in severe dire straits if I hadn't been wheeled in then.

It turned out that I had a huge obstruction in my bladder – a condition that medical doctors would use to describe a growth or cancer of any kind. Furthermore, the emergency ultrasound that I had done prior to being taken into the emergency ward signalled that this obstruction needed to be removed, and that it could possibly be invading other parts of my internals. I had absolutely no idea what was transpiring, and no one in my family could fathom the pain that I was enduring. Finally, the doctor ordered a pain killer injection, the wonder drug called Pethidine, the same drug that was normally administered to patients who went into labour, and there was an immediate sense of relief.

Upon securing my debilitating state, I was asked to fill out some forms and needed to be admitted. This was the first time in my life that I needed to a "drip" inserted - a line which was placed in my veins to facilitate the administration of fluids, medicine, or drugs. I remember abusing the nurse who was inserting the drip because she took almost five attempts to get it right and I really gave her a hard time. It was then that I realized how bad the situation was, not because of the drip or pain killers, but upon observing the look on my doctor's face when he came in to inform us that I needed surgery. I was just about to turn thirty two, and felt that I was too young to be facing this dilemma. Still, it wasn't a death sentence, and I was optimistic amidst the fear that was prevailing in my bones. I had to put up a brave front as I was admitted into a single room. It was like a hotel room, and the only thing I did to comfort myself was to ask Ruben who was also with me to get me a packet of cigarettes – unbelievable as it sounds, this was exactly what I needed then. After polishing up a plate of Hokkien Mee and a cold milo, I sneaked into the bathroom and had a few drags of Benson and Hedges. At this juncture, I was operating on a "no pain" mode, I was absolutely pain free and it seemed that I would be laughing my way through the ordeal. Little did I realize that the pethidine had kicked in and in layman's terms, I was flying! It was time for me to get ready for the procedure the following morning and Dr. Shanmugan was going to perform a "Cystoscopy". The "Journal of Medicine" describes it as follows:

"Cystoscopy (sis-TOS-kuh-pee) is a procedure used to see inside your urinary bladder and urethra — the tube that carries urine from your bladder to the outside of your body. During a cystoscopy procedure, the doctor uses a hollow tube (cystoscopy) equipped with a lens to carefully examine the lining of your bladder and your urethra. The cystoscope is then inserted into the urethra and slowly advances into the bladder".

This procedure was done under general anaesthesia, and my doctor was able to detect a very large mass on the bladder wall. The procedure enabled him to remove some tissue sample from the affected area, known as a biopsy. The sample was then sent for further investigation. The surgery was over in less than thirty minutes, and I was wheeled out of the operating theatre. I remember clearly that I had this insane urge to urinate and the sensation was like my penis was on fire. I kept saying, "I need to pee, I need to pee" and the attending nurse said, okay, pee! I thought to myself, what? – "pee here", on the bed, and then I realized what had happened. The procedure also required a tube to be inserted into the opening of the urethra - a catheter was inserted and at the end of it was a urinary bag, which collected the waste. I panicked for a moment as all this was new to me. I had never seen anything like this before; much less endure the pain and embarrassment of having one in me. The burning sensation was due to spasms which was apparently normal.

I relieved myself, checking every so often to see if I had wet my bed, but thankfully it was all under control. Still, I had this damn tube in me, in my penile entry, and I immediately felt that I had been robbed of my manhood! Yes, I went that far, and this time, I was not hallucinating from the drugs or any other opioids – it was all me, my mind was beginning to wonder. I hadn't done any research into this type of a procedure and I had absolutely no inclination of what a bladder obstruction was, so all this was "Greek" to me. In all honesty, the doctors and nurses had no other way of relating the news to me and my family but to come out and say it; - there was a possibility that I may have a tumour down there! Oh Jesus Christ! This can't be right. I endured five days of hospitalization, after which the catheter was removed to my great relief, and I was discharged. This was just the beginning of what I was about to experience.

The biopsy was sent to Singapore for further investigation, and under the recommendation of my uncle, I was referred to a Dr. E. C. Tan at Mt Elizabeth Hospital. Dr. Tan was a noble urologist, whose patients came from all walks of life, many of whom were from overseas. He was a gentle fellow and had a wonderful sense of humour while he displayed tact and calmness in his approach. Prior to visiting him, I was asked to undergo another procedure, a CT scan at the specialist centre. I remember this day like it was yesterday. My brother, Aunt Gana Jegadeva, my sister, mother and a very good friend Satish Krishnan, all accompanied me for this procedure. Satish was a close family friend, more like a brother, who drove me and my family from Johor Bahru across the causeway. It was later revealed to me that a prior discussion had taken place between my late uncle and the doctor in Johor Bahru about my family history of cancer, and it was brought to the attention of Dr Tan that my father, his father, mother, host of cousins, and first born men in the Kularatnam clan and relatives, had all passed away from colon cancer at a very young age.

Naturally, this conversation never took place in my presence; I was operating under the notion that I had, at the worst case, a bout of kidney stones or a urinary tract infection. Dr. Shanmugam from Johor Bahru was convinced that there was no indication of cancer of any kind, let alone cancer in my bladder. Still, this was all news to me and my family. So, like most of the times when I was faced with some ordeal or another, this was now a new day, with a deep seated sense of apprehension, and my unconscious mind was about to clash head on with an imminent state of consciousness. I was called in to undergo the CT scan and it was all over in twenty minutes.

Finally, after a long wait, the epic setting and dilemma unfolded when the results of the scan were revealed to us. At some point of my consciousness and in the development of my inner most thoughts, reality struck. I knew that I was not well, but what I was about to hear was unfathomable! This was by no means an extension of my imagination. This was just too obscure and esoteric, and it was just a matter of time when Professor E.C. Tan called us into his room and delivered the news. I had an inoperable form of bladder cancer. The mass that was detected in the walls of the ladder was malignant and at thirty two years of age, I was about to face death in the face. There were no surgical options available, and all that I could do was to undergo vigorous and aggressive chemotherapy. I had limited time left on my hands.

You can probably imagine the reaction from my mother who broke down uncontrollably. Thankfully, my aunt was there to console her. I on the other hand, was still in shock, but took the news the best way I knew how, that was to weigh my options and talked to as many experts whom the family knew on this subject matter. This was alienating me from my inner self, and all I wanted to do was to get out of there, out of the hospital as far as I could. We left the clinic in a state of utter alienation and not to mention, confusion of the highest order. Surely there were other options to consider, we asked? On the way down to the car park, my brother, who had been quiet all this time asked if I was okay, to which I answered yes, in an affirmative fashion, while holding on to shreds of my life as it was being torn apart right in front of me.

The news of my diagnosis went all around the country, and to make things more difficult, I had the most difficult task of informing my company and Rose, that I had bladder cancer. We had been together for almost seven years now, and all this time, Rose had been the pillar of strength for me personally and emotionally, especially when I had lost my grandfather and grandmother during the earlier years. My uncle from Australia, my mother's brother, Dr. Meyhandan, a Cardiac Physician, had wondered about the diagnosis and got on the phone with my uncle in Ipoh and some other doctor friends that he had kept in contact with over the years. According to experts at that time, this diagnosis was somewhat syncretic, and seemed to contradict most of the case studies that had been done on bladder cancer, and it was apparent that it seemed rather odd for a young thirty two year old to have such a debilitating diagnosis. The recovery on the outset seemed to be weakened by the fact that surgery was not an option. As I kept looking at the CT Scans and the films showing the mass along the bladder, I took on a look of disbelief and wondered if this was it, was my life all over at the age of thirty two?

I quickly asked for a second opinion within the surgical fraternity in Singapore and Malaysia, and told myself that death or dying was not an option. I was too young, I wanted a family, I wanted to get married, have children and I had a life ahead of me, to live by, and to fulfil all my dreams and aspirations. I wondered then and there if I could beat this cancer diagnosis with a strong will to live and deal with this with all my might. I needed a spirited approach which would transcend all parameters of a normal state of comprehension, but I had no idea where to start. I knew one thing for sure, that it was apparent that I had enough internal and external factors to heal and walk down that path of recovery. The funny thing is I was already looking ahead by planning what colour bandana I should wear when I would go bald from chemotherapy, where would I be staying and would I be fortunate enough to have a sea front view so that the ocean would seem to be a perfect companion. Or should I just sit in silence and stare into the dim light, hoping that this would help to personify the virtues of healing.

Internally, I was a mess, but externally, I was calm and cool as a cat, and after we had spent what felt like a lifetime in this sudden environment of uncertainty, I needed to come to terms that I had cancer, it was now my turn after my father had it, who in fact left us two months short of his 50th birthday. As I'm writing this chapter, I'm three weeks away from my 50th birthday! It's probably appropriate that I share my sister's "musings" and her contribution to my journey thus far.

My sister Priya Darshini writes:-

As I decided to embark on this writing, I wondered what would be the best title....after many trials....I decided to quote the mystique in my life... "SADGHURU" ...*MUSINGS OF A SISTER...*

MUSINGS OF A SISTER

I do not remember the childhood memories of us playing.

Though…I remember the days of "GULI" (playing marbles) and the cricket matches that you used to be engrossed in…

I remember the day when life made a turnaround for all of us…

I remember the day you walked out of the terminal and saw papa…

I remember the tears of death, the joys of studying, the memories of passion,

The shock of your own destiny….

Most of all I remember the time when it was all-silent.

When every waking moment was a miracle

For months I have been contemplating what to share with you, my eldest brother, the pillar of our family, the prodigal son…. as you turn fifty…..and finally I decided that I would share my memories.

As a younger sister living with two brothers…….in the beginning it was always fascinating. I always wanted your toys, your bravery and passion for life. STILL….

Papa's attempts to provide me with girly toys never ceased to amuse me…. I wanted what my brothers had and that was GUNS & GULI!!!!

Perinanna, as an older brother is called in the Tamil language, was always the pillar of strength for our family mostly for my mother - amma.

He never failed to always be there for us as we were growing up. Though as a younger sibling I am sure I was not that appreciative of his "fatherly ways"

Besides, who ever listens!

The day that still haunts my memory is the day my father left us... is the moment Perinanna stepped in and decided our family would still prosper and progress despite papa being gone.

During those years, anna was always the father figure to me....he was the pillar for my mother. I do not think she would have survived without his support.

Life does not always play the game that you want...hence the moment came when illness took over his life and our family needed to look within to be strong...my mother had many moments when life almost failed her.....but her love for her son and her determination to ensure that anna made it to see another birthday... gave her that inner strength.

My brother.....there are many words to describe you.

There are many incidents in my life where it could have turned out differently...

In the end ISWARA played a hand and we are all still here together.... respectful cohesiveness might be the best way to describe this journey of ours.

He stands strong,
He has fought his battles,
He has loved with zest,
He has cried in anguish,
He has parted in anger,
He has returned in humility
He has thrived to look within
His journey is still untold.

Happy 50th birthday my dear brother. Through the years, you have always been in my heart. The laughter, tears, anguish, anger, pain, frustration, humour and spiritual exchanges have been internally rewarding.

My sister and her husband, Ruben

Though all this could be condensed into a running narrative, people in my family needed to absorb the news in small pieces and soft doses. I, on the other hand, needed to deal with it quickly. This was an independent episode and yet, I couldn't help but feel that people were already planning my funeral. Think about it, bladder cancer, inoperable, chemotherapy, and hope for the best – that's simply too insightful for anyone to think otherwise. It meant, go home and get your affairs in order. You've just re-visited your family history!

9

The death sentence

"Facing mortality is easier than you think, if there's such a thing as an extrasensory vision"

So far as this episode goes, my immediate family, extended family of relatives and their relatives and not to mention the entourage of family friends, were all informed of my condition. Now, I needed to tell the folks at work exactly what had transpired and at this very moment, I went into my room and held myself together. Speaking to the bosses about the diagnosis was tough and I cried uncontrollably, perhaps the only time that I actually displayed an emotional response to the situation. They were speechless; more like dumbfounded upon hearing the news, and all I could hear was "Oh My God"! There was nothing much else that they could possibly say at the time but I knew deep down that they were very sad to hear about their star performer being gravely ill.

This was an immensely difficult moment, and I had already decided that I would put up a brave front in the presence of my immediate family, while realizing that I had no time to be righteous about the episode. I literally had to wait out a death sentence and presumably everything in my "to do list" needed to be suspended and placed on a waiting list. I came to terms with the fact that if I wanted to get over this, I needed to have an action plan – but this was no ordinary plan. You see cancer in the circle of my family life and its history meant death, and at an early age. So here I was, at thirty two, facing the ultimate sentence. I was on death row, and the only consolation was that I would be on this waiting list in the comfort of my own home, and not in an '*Alcatraz*' like setting.

Now I had to get to work and I had no idea where to start. I dug deep within my consciousness and came up with a statement declaring war against this illness. I mentioned about my relationship with time in the previous chapter, and I fully understood that the remaining time I had left would only mean something if I filled it up with a purpose, not leaving it empty and allowing it to burden my existence. I acknowledged the past and how the chain of events had led to this very day, and I set out to acquire another day, day in and day out, twenty four hours at a time. So where was the present moment I asked? This was obviously a statement about the imminent future, which at that point seemed bleak and empty, inhospitable and charmless, and I kind of related this to the past and thought that this could be the present moment. It seemed logical to think so but there was a problem, and it was beyond having cancer, it was about dealing with the irreplaceable truth - I was going to die. But if you have been following this journey thus far, there are a few things in life that I cannot tolerate and one of them is failure, and now, I felt like I was about to compromise for what could possibly be a really bright future. If only I had the vision to see beyond that point? Yes, I needed an extrasensory vision!

This episode was a wake-up call and I took full responsibility for both the successes and failures in my life, but this was not what I had desired, this was not on my wish list and therefore, I was not about to compromise on an underdeveloped potential. Setting this aside for a moment, I summed up my life very quickly and in all the thirty two years of living, I realized that I was the sum total of the choices that I had made and perhaps it was time for me to pay for my sins. However righteous or otherwise, there were upcoming choices that I needed to make, and decisions that I needed to come to terms with, and it was at that very moment, sitting alone in my room, that I decided that I was going to scrutinize each and every choice or decision that would be forthcoming. Therein lies the quality of my future life, and I was confident that even in the shortest time left, I was going to make it meaningful and opulent to say the least.

This was not about an assessment of myself, the before and after diagnosis, but more of a self-realizing prophecy, one that would justify all the means necessary for me to fight this dreaded illness that had consumed half of my previous generation. This was about the 'mother of all battles', and it was obvious that I needed to have a new approach towards my personal growth, one which I had mentioned in the opening brief to this book. The remaining time would be my responsibility, and while I knew that in my quest to nurture my personal growth, there would be problems at every turn, fear at every corner, but I reaffirmed my belief in myself and my faith in my creator, and promised myself that whatever I would feel from then on would only be a positive charge in my existence, much like an increasing shadow of my own growth process. I asked myself a question, can this be a real adventure? Let's see what transpires...... The essence of my diagnosis was now real; this was no longer a theory or some manifestation in my mind. This was happening, and as the day quietened down,

I retired to bed to reflect once more on what had been presented before me. My sister and Ruben came into the room and we had a quiet moment together, I can't really remember what was said but I told them both that I was going to be fine.

It has been said that we can either choose to tap into our extrasensory vision when everything around us seems to be falling apart and mine was seriously being tested. This was now 1996, the year had already moved past March, and catastrophe was about to be revealed, this time on a magnitude beyond comprehension. It was time to look into the treatment modalities before me and at the insistence of my late uncle, who kept harping about the fact that it was rare for a thirty two year old to have bladder cancer; I decided to find out more about this diagnosis. The war within was about to erupt – meet Professor Abu Rauff, Consultant Surgeon at Mt. Elizabeth Hospital, Singapore. The good Professor agreed to meet with me and after a series of invasive tests, sticking his middle finger up my orifice, which felt like sodomy of the highest form, there it was, an apparent growth at the base of the rectum.

Professor Rauff said that he could feel the growth at the tip of his fingers, and as much as I wanted to *'knock his bloody block off'*, I was more afraid of passing out on the examination table in his clinic. The pain from this procedure, which is medically known as a digital examination, was unimaginable; having someone twist and turn their finger up my anus was unbearable. Still, I sucked it all in, took a deep breath, and it was over before it even began, while pandemonium certainly belonged to this moment. I certainly belonged to that very moment because it was revealed to me even before any tests were done that there was a possibility of a large tumour nesting in my anal passage, closer to the rectum.

I remember when I had first arrived in Singapore and the Prime Minister then, Mr Lee Kwan Yew had revealed to the public that his eldest son, Lee Hsien Loong, had lymphoma and at the same time, President Ong Teng Cheong had a tumour in his colon.

I joked about this and candidly said that "one was a pain in the neck, while the other was a pain in the arse"!! – referring to the cancer that is. Well, I certainly had one, deep in my arse and it was suggested that I undergo a colonoscopy to explore this further. According to the medical dictionary, a colonoscopy is *"the endoscopic examination of the large bowel and the distal part of the small bowel with a CCD camera or a fiber optic camera on a flexible tube passed through the anus. It can provide a visual diagnosis (e.g. ulceration, polyps) and grants the opportunity for biopsy or removal of suspected colorectal cancer lesions".*

This was sodomy on a grand scale, and whatever anyone tells you, it's larger than you think. First, the attending physician inserts a huge probe into your anus to dilate the opening, and then the flexible tube is inserted. Before the procedure, I asked if I could remain conscious because I wanted to watch the procedure on the big screen, and the fellow who attended to me said it was possible, and that I would need a mild sedative to ease the pain and discomfort. Discomfort!! My arse!!! This was not just discomforting but hugely invasive but since I asked for it, my wish was granted. I know, I'm a sucker for punishment, but I felt that it was necessary. During the procedure, I was able to converse fluently with the physician, so that meant that whatever sedative that he had administered was certainly not doing the job, or perhaps my conscious mind was overriding the entire episode. Along the way, I watched my intestinal tract being probed, scrapped and prodded at every possible angle, and as the tube was about to exit the anal passage, there it was, a massive growth, flaming red like a volcano about to erupt! This damn thing had been hiding behind the anal passage, lodged in between the rectum and anus, and it was not looking good.

At that very moment, I was enraged with anger, fear and utter disbelief at what I had just witnessed and said to myself, bladder and rectum? What's next? I immediately recognized the crisis at hand and realized that this was no longer a mere urinary tract infection, this was full blown cancer, and from what I had gathered from the physician, it was a late stage cancer, since it had already extended beyond the intestinal walls and onto the bladder. Anxiety, coupled with apprehension, and an overwhelming and powerful sense of fear consumed me all at once, and I believe I swore at the physician in a flowery manner. My immediate reaction was utter panic, and I lashed out at everyone in the examination room and told them all that they were prophets of doom, and that they would never be able to have a decent nights' sleep from then on. I was coming back to haunt them every day, until they too succumbed to the same fate. In all my might, and as drastic as it sounds, I promised to yield a powerful force that would create pain and misery in their lives. Their reaction was not what I had expected, they were apparently well trained to deal with patients like myself and probably realized that the magnitude of discovering cancer at an early age was something quite unlike anything else, and that to grasp this ordeal all at once would be pushing the limits of normal behaviour.

Ralph Waldo Emerson said that "we acquire the strength of the thing we have to overcome" and yet I found no strength in me at that moment to overcome my imminent fear of dying from cancer. I knew that my life up to that point was full of challenging situations, and yet, I opted to act in an irrational way, instead of reaching within my soul to seek for some solace and guidance.

The thing is, I had no apparent faith left, in anything or in anyone, and I had no clear options before me as to how I was supposed to react. Right up to this moment, with the exception of my short outburst when I found myself helpless and alone at the Y.M.C.A in Auckland and later on in Puteri Specialist Hospital, Johor Bahru, I was clever to hide my worry and pain from my own conscious awareness, and even to the people around me. I would often lie to myself and operated on the assumption that everything was in good order, and this huge misapprehension before me was somewhat manageable.

There was obviously a lot of pain that I had tucked away in a litter-bag which was filled with drama, conflict and indecisiveness. As turbulent as this appeared to be, my thoughts and levels of tension seemed to be travelling in opposite directions, and needless to say, I was ever so doubtful that I was going to survive this diagnosis. Back at the ward in the surgical wing, my family had gathered around my two bedded room, and we were waiting for Professor Rauff to come in to deliver the verdict. Since I had not eaten anything the whole day, I was obviously famished and was craving for some food. It was dinner time, and at around 6pm that evening, I tucked into some hospital food.

While the serving of rice and chicken was somewhat palatable, the news that I was about to receive was certainly not on the same scale. Professor Rauff was a man whose bedside manners was left to be desired, so when he came in to deliver the news in the company of some other doctors, they were unfazed by his approach, while my family and I were shocked and aghast at the way he spoke about the prognosis. In one simple sentence, he delivered the verdict and said that I had stage four rectum cancer with secondaries in the bladder, and he was somewhat emotionless!

I almost choked on my food, but I had to refrain from "throwing up", so I stopped eating. The only choice left was to remain silent while he spoke. We had done some research into the brilliance of this Professor, and it was related to us that he was indeed a very capable surgeon, and that he had, in his tenure as a consultant surgeon, saved many lives, most of them with stage two or three cancer, but not many with stage four. Still, he was the best doctor available, and I was willing to endure his seemingly brash attitude and not so charming bedside manners if it meant that he was going to give me a second chance at life. He was quick to explain the treatment plan - I needed twenty four rounds of intensive radiation therapy, surgery after that, and chemotherapy of at least twelve cycles, and then I would need to wait and see, and there would be no guarantees.

So now, this sentence had taken on a new dimension - all the invasive procedures seemed imperative, and there was nothing certain ahead. The road was winding, and there was no light at the end of the tunnel. At this moment, my attention was drawn to the rest of the folks in the room. Some were quiet, some were crying, while I was motionless. It was as if I was staring at the dashboard of my car, and all the lights were blinking, alarms were sounding off, and the horn was blaring for no apparent reason. I needed to look for that special switch in my head, the one that I would reach for to flick and turn off all the noise and disruption simultaneously, and make this doctor invisible.

It didn't happen, naturally, as there was more news to come. I needed a colostomy bag which would collect all my bodily waste from the surgery which would divert my colon out to the abdominal wall. Huh! WHAT? NO WAY! NO, ABSOLUTELY NOT! And this was said while I was eating!!! This was when, for the first time since this ordeal started, that I broke down into pieces and wailed as if I had just lost someone close to me, and it sounded pretty much like the way I wailed when my father died. My immediate thought then was for someone to shoot me. In fact, there's a story behind this, as I recalled a Television Program that I had watched sometime back. The sportsman in this program who had a similar situation needed a colostomy, and his girlfriend told him that she would relieve him of his pain and suffering if he allowed her to shoot him. I remember mentioning to Ruben some time back, and I can't recall why I said this, that if ever anything like this were to happen to me, I would sanction the act of him shooting me dead. Premonition perhaps! I really don't know, but now this was a calamity, a catastrophe and an absolute disaster that was being presented right before my eyes.

I was rather convinced that all the drama and confusion in my life was a result of a tumultuous state of mind. This was basically the sum total of everything that I had done in the past, and as I slumped into the hospital bed, I knew very well that the truth was finally out, "we reap what we sow". I just wanted to die, then and there, because to me, there was no reason to live. Not in the condition that was expected of me, and even more so for the reason that there were no guarantees that I was going to survive. Remember when I had my episode with the unwanted visitor? Well, turmoil was back, and I believed then that it was contagious, and my condition was being internalized further by this insane feeling of rage, fear, disbelief, and utter disappointment. I felt like I had let myself and everyone else down, and even though I was clinging on to some hope of coming out of this ordeal alive, I was looking at the certainty of compromising.

As the news slowly sunk in, I came to terms with the fact that this was a temporary ordeal, and with some help and even some divine intervention, surviving this diagnosis could be a possibility.

I needed baby steps, first to recover from the shock, gather my thoughts, and whatever strength I had left, drawing on some silent strength that I had tucked away in a safety vault in case of an emergency, and then look towards some guidance and positive support from my family. That night, after washing up, Rose and I spoke at great length and she decided to sit with me for a while as my immediate family left the room to get some food and some much needed rest.

Rose had been a stoic character all this while, and she would always appear with a wide smile, full of zest, and never once did she show any signs of being affected by my condition. On that day, as I was about to say goodnight, she hugged me and cried, we cried together and it felt awful, really awful, but it had to happen, and I thought, better at that moment than later, when the journey ahead was about to get more and more intense. Another drama in my life was the fact that my mother had not come to terms with the fact that I was seeing a Muslim girl. This was a difficult time for her, and although I understood my mother's perspective, Rose was steadfast in her approach towards our relationship. Any other woman would have left, leaving skid marks, but not Rose, she stood firm and decided that she was going to help me through this ordeal. Where on earth did this woman come from? What had I done to deserve such an amazing person in my life? Well, we hugged each other for a moment and she looked at me and said, 'we will get over this'. I had a blank expression on my face as all this was unfolding, but I kept clinging on to the fact that there was an undeniable force to be reckoned with, and maybe, just maybe, I will prevail.

There was a new game plan now, and I began my search after saying goodnight to everyone. I began an exploration with myself and what was left of me. I still had all my organs intact and I was alive and seemed quite well, despite a twenty five kilogram weight reduction. Yes, it was clear that I looked like a malnourished child! I experienced some resistance as I fell into a deep sleep that night. Perhaps it was time for me to rest as well.

The next day and the days after that, scores and scores of visitors came to see me. I had friends, clients, and even old man Hassan, who would visit me on his way back from the bank along Orchard Road. He often came to see me when no one else was around, and we would talk for a brief moment. I remember one morning - he had tears in his eyes, and he commented on how much weight I had lost. I must have been a large fellow prior to this ordeal. This was surreal and at the same time troubling, because the old man was also not that well. I really treasured his visits because it always gave me some hope that I would one day, be back at work with my Oriental babies. There was hope, I was sure of it.

Doctors and nurses would visit me on a daily basis, and in between the visits from my family, I was slowly starting to come to terms with my condition, and that I needed a colostomy. A mutual friend of the Hassan's family visited me and mentioned that The Queen Mother had one, and not to mention some celebrities and famous singers. I thought to myself, if they can live with it, so can I. As much as I detected some hope, I was still unsure but there was a sense of relief. I began to ask a lot of questions and my aunt from Australia had sent me some literature on surviving cancer and even a CD on living with a colostomy. I spent my days and nights in the hospital ward reading up on the subject matter and realized that there was an entire world out there, of people from various walks of life who were referred to as '*Ostomates*' – as in someone who had an ostomy as a result of a surgical operation to create an opening in the body for the discharge of body wastes. This was something else, and I needed to connect with them somehow. For now, it was time to go home and I was discharged after a five day admission. It was time to see the oncologist whose principle goal was to put me on a rigorous radiation treatment program.

There was a short waiting period of two weeks before I was required to report for radiation therapy. I took this opportunity to reflect and re-create my mission to heal and motivate myself personally, not only as a means of surviving, but to a greater extent, a means of dealing with certain value creations that I had employed all through my life, to the point of being diagnosed with cancer. I wanted that special internalized experience of connecting the dots, crossing the t's and dotting the i's - I wanted the experience that would still leave the sanctity of my life intact, and without compromising a shred of humanity that I had left. The only way I was going to achieve any of this was to go back to work and I did that, almost immediately after being discharged from hospital. I needed to be surrounded by my rugs, the people; I needed the spirit to belong and to exist beyond the realm of comprehension.

I spoke to the bosses and they were thrilled to say the least. It had been a while since I was last seen at work, so naturally, the immediate reaction to my visit was met with caution and worry all rolled up into a nice scroll. They of course, commented on my weight loss again - I wasn't allowed to carry any rugs, let alone pick any up from the floor, roll them or fold them. It was about this time that the company had purchased their very first personal computer with internet connectivity. This was the dial up version, we had no broadband then, no wireless internet, but nevertheless, it was a moment of new discoveries and tremendous possibilities. I manoeuvred the 'mouse' for the very first time and the cursor was going all over the small fourteen inch screen that was in front of me. As I cursed at it, we laughed together as to how stupid I was when my superior's eight year old son was seen blazing his way through the computer rather effortlessly. With the help of this boy, I worked on the computer, searching for information on cancer, on living with a colostomy and there was even porn on the "world wide web". Wow! There was light at the end of the tunnel now, for sure. Porn on the internet meant that we didn't need to sneak our dirty magazines in and out of the showroom. All we needed to do was to turn the screen around and magic appeared right before our eyes. Yes, life was back and going back to work every day meant a great deal - there was some motivation waiting for me. I had great colleagues then, I must say.

A week went by and it was time to prepare myself mentally for the treatment ahead. My aunt, Dr. Rani Meyhandan (Dr. Meyhandan's wife) had sent me a book by Ian Gawler, who authored "you can conquer cancer". Ian Gawler was an exceptional man with an exceptional story about recovering and healing. His discourse was not only about cancer, but about life's choices, and it was an inspiration to read. He wrote his account on the first step he took when he found out that he had cancer and posed a question; "do we want to take responsibility for our own condition?" The discussion here was not about facing our own mortality or trying on the extrasensory hat. It was about the creation of a total and committed state of mind – perhaps seen as an extension of that extrasensory vision that I needed. I had already asked the question about the terminal stage of my illness to which I received no reply from the doctors. So the only question left was if I really wanted to get better or to give in to cancer.

There were grounds for an increased state of belief – and I really believed that I was going to get better. However, this needed to be reaffirmed on many levels, and across many channels within the core of my living being. This needed to function as a unit and an entity without barriers. I had to eliminate all the elements of doubt first, and then tackle the illness head on, making this course of action the primary focus and the preferred objective. Easier said than done you might say, but believe me when I say that there was no doubt in my mind, that even though I was about to face a rather short life span, the remaining years were not going to be filled with misery. Pain was inevitable but suffering was a choice and I was not about to make that decision to suffer. And so, began the journey into the radiation therapy room. The healing had begun.

10

Reclaiming my sense of purpose and my birth right

"There are no answers, only choices"

If you think that talking about this is a little premature, then think again! One of my earliest experience in dealing with cancer is that when you least expect it, someone will come up to you and say, "Dhush, the world doesn't owe you a living just because you have cancer". Get the point!! So yes, that's true to a certain extent, but how would they know when they hadn't been in my shoes! So as much as I despised this type of attitude, I also realized that I needed to stop feeling sorry and it was time to kick things into high gear. So perhaps some people were actually doing me a favour by indirectly telling me to take matters into my own hands. In the previous chapter, I spoke about Ian Gawler and his approach where he basically formed a relationship between his medical treatment, his doctors and his will power to overcome his ordeal. I realized immediately that this was what I needed to do. While my doctors would be the central figure, my job was to accept responsibility, and instead of blaming the whole world for my sorry state of affairs and feeling bitter about it, I needed to balance my weakness and the defensive behaviour of the medical personnel.

At that point, I had an epiphany, that cancer was an enigma, sent by the forces of nature to test me. This experience of a sudden and striking realization that it was more than a philosophical discovery was becoming clear to me. This was not a moment of glory, and certainly not what I had been waiting for. Ironically, it didn't surprise me when people from my inner circle were not entirely surprised that I had been struck down by this debilitating illness, it was sort of expected, but the only surprise was that it had struck so early in my life. So you see, I had discovered a new sense of belonging to the universe, and the only way that I was going to prevail in my journey of healing was to understand the fact that while there were no clear answers, no guarantees, I needed to make a decision, and that there were choices to be made. I had cancer so far up my arse that if it spat, it would come out of my mouth!!

We're all familiar with Thomas Edison's famous quote that "genius is one percent inspiration and ninety-nine percent perspiration". This by no means indicated that we needed to suffer in order to maximize our potential. In my situation, I needed to make a choice as to how I wanted to maximize my healing process. No doubt, radiation therapy was only the beginning, but it was also a means to the end of the journey ahead, and I had already decided that failure was not an option. It was time to summon the steel inside me. I suppose I wanted to impress myself, but I hadn't realized it then. Looking at the immediate task ahead, I decided to put this into a movie like context where there would be a hero, a villain and a traitor. Needless to say, I was the hero, cancer was the villain and radiation therapy was the traitor. Why? Well, radiation therapy is not the ultimate solution or a quick fix to the problem, and it often gave out false alarms that if one were to undergo its treatment, cancer would disappear. While it would inevitably shrink the large tumour that was nesting in my rectum, it also meant damaging the surrounding tissues no matter how localized the treatment would have been.

In this movie, the hero needed to make a decision before going any further, and that was clear from the beginning. The hero needed to remove all the obstacles, real or imaginary, that had been placed before him by various factors. These factors would seem to be a huge distraction, and it was the hero's ultimate game plan to pay absolutely no attention to these distractions. Then, the hero needed to acknowledge the villain which was the illness, and it was the hero's job to place its vantage point beyond recognizable limits – this meant that whatever negative aspects or feelings that he would have felt being emitted by the villain needed to be placed in a vault and locked up for good. In doing so, the hero would understand the meaning of the illness, which was merely a condition with restrictions that were being imposed upon him, and in order to move forward, day by day, these restrictions needed to be broken down into pieces.

I was recovering in Johor Bahru while waiting for my call to begin radiation therapy and since I was able to move freely, I decided to take this opportunity to go back to work as often as I could. In this exercise, I was able to catch up on some correspondence with clients, do more research on radiation therapy and undertook a small assignment to deliver a class on the art of recognizing and appreciating antique rugs from The Province of Azerbaijan, North West Iran. This was an area that had caught my attention very early in the trade, and I began to specialize in this collection of rugs, which also brought about a greater understanding of the silk-road. According to Judy Bonavia, who authored a fantastic book on this subject, the silk- road was named in the middle of the 19th Century by the German Scholar, Baron Ferdinand von Richthofen. The Silk Road was perhaps the greatest East-West trade route, and vehicle for cross cultural exchange.

I read extensively on the trading pattern of the travellers who applied themselves across the vast plains and in most hostile and inhospitable conditions, realizing that they must have endured great discomfort along the way. This enabled me to divert my attention away from the anxiety of having to endure my illness and the upcoming treatment which I was told, would be rough and very unpleasant. During my lecture, I delivered with deceptive simplicity to arrive at a confident presentation, while harbouring my fear and conflict of having to battle cancer. All along, I was faced with two factions of the prognosis, one that was evidently clear on the path of recovery, and the other, heading downhill towards an early death. I reminded myself of the promise that I had made when I was first diagnosed with bladder cancer, and decided that battling this illness would mean placing it in a context worth living, and I simply refused to look at this as a means to a dignified death, but more of a way to live a dignified life.

That was it; this illness was not going to take me away at the age of thirty two. My work was a blessing in disguise because I realized that I used the intensity of colour and design from the beautiful rugs that I was fortunate enough to have handled and studied – to create a narrative of a personal guide to my daily affairs. This relationship may be difficult for some to understand at this juncture, but let me assure you that by the end of this journey, I will reveal how it personified a sense of relief towards all the problems that I was about to be faced with. Strangely, I had dialogues with my rugs, and this was seen as an act of searching deep within the mind, body, and spirit and it was an appeal, desperate at times, for some wisdom that needed to be sought after. I searched within the minds of the people who were responsible for creating these magical pieces of art, and spoke to them subconsciously. Their language, disposition and sheer will to transcend beyond all adversity was an eye opener to my inner psyche. I'll expand more on the brilliance of rugs of this category later on in this book, but for now, let's begin with the immediate task at hand - radiation therapy.

Athar Hamid, my boss at Hassan's, insisted that I stay with him and his family during this difficult time, and since I wasn't married then, my girlfriend Rose would visit me on a daily basis to check on me and spend some quality time. My mother too, stayed with me in Hamid's home, and it was an incredible act of kindness on the part of his family to have taken us into their space at a time when the situation was so fragile. His children were all very young then - the eldest boy was around twelve years old while the youngest daughter was just a few months old. There were five kids in all, and they were like my little brothers and sisters. Neelofur, Athar's wife, was a dynamic and head strong woman, who was just a couple of years older than me. She kept the family unit together as mother, educator, care giver, wife, friend, sister, and went out of her way to ensure that both my mother and I were completely at ease in her home.

If ever there was a moment of doubt in my mind that I was never going to make it through this ordeal, Neelo would set me straight, and instilled upon the need to be positive and strong. She was a god loving woman, and encouraged me to adhere to the will of god. My plea for help was immediate and personal, and yet, the response I received from this remarkable family was not only universal, but timeless. I can't put this in words any more than

I already have, but to say that I will forever be indebted to this family is an understatement. They kept reminding me that they were there for me, with no reservations or conditions, and all I needed to do was to fight, with all my might.

Radiation therapy was brutal. Neelofur (Athar Hamid's wife), would drive me to Mt. Elizabeth hospital every day for the treatment and then we would go straight home, where a special meal, specially prepared to cater to a well-balanced diet was served, together with a vegetarian spread for my mother. On some days, I would ask to be taken to the showroom for a change in scenery and to be with my babies, my rugs, but the strain and drain would soon begin to show. Radiation therapy was taking its toll on my body and the skin around my lower back, hips, lower abdomen and pelvic region would show signs of literally being burnt, even to the extent of the outer layer of my skin showing signs of decay. I bled profusely when I needed to go to the toilet and the weight loss was becoming more and more noticeable.

With the treatment almost completing its course, I began to experience a fair bit of fear, I was afraid of the next step, which was the surgery. However, I needed to conquer this fear, but had no will or spirit to begin the battle, let alone think about anything else. This was a period of utmost uncertainty, and I would be faced with the dilemma of having to come to terms with a terminal stage cancer. My closest friends would visit me every day and in the evenings, we would sit in the living room on one of Athar's personal collection of Persian Rugs and just converse, about anything and everything, often mundane at times.

One of the talks that we would have revolved around the concept of fear and I was told that fear can actually be a good thing. It's a biological instinct that prevents us from doing stupid things that might inflict harm. However, fear is not always rational and not always healthy. In my case, fear could have prevented me from inflicting anymore harm on myself with overpowering negative thoughts, but it also held me back from the chance of recognizing the pain of a crushed ego and the exhilaration of victory and success. I did mention before that I strongly felt that I had let myself and everyone else down. As the weeks progressed, radiation therapy was coming to an end and amidst all the drama and turmoil, I completed all the twenty four sessions and managed to endure the after effects the best way I knew how. Like all the times that I had been placed in a compromising situation, I would perform checks and balances on my personality, and present it to the next phase of my life. In doing so, it gave me the tenacity to claim a bit of my self-worth and dignity, my basic birth right to function and live with a purpose, instead of merely existing. I needed to take myself out of isolation and it was time to have my very first major surgery in all my thirty two years of living.

There wasn't even a slimmest fraction of doubt that the cancer was indeed aggressive, but when I finally visited Professor Rauff to check on my progress and to confirm the date for the surgery, I was pleasantly surprised to discover that my tumour had shrunk considerably. This time, Professor Rauff was really upbeat and a lot more jovial than he was when we first met. Needless to say, I was finger sodomised again when he performed another rectal examination, and it was confirmed that the base of the tumour was not so prevalent after radiation therapy. I thought to myself that the traitor in the movie may have had a change of heart perhaps. Still, I knew the damage had already been done to the rest of my surrounding internal organs but I had no other choice, I needed to come to terms with this and we finally fixed the date for the surgery on the 9th of July, 1996.

After spending almost two months at Watten View in the Hamid residence, we said our goodbyes and it was time to go back to Johor Bahru. However, something remarkable happened, just one day before we were about to leave. Rose had come to visit me after I had received the prognosis from Professor Rauff. Later that night, my mother commented to Neelo that she was still unhappy about my seeing Rose, and that she was not prepared to sanction the relationship. Apparently from what I was told, Neelo had some exchange of words with my mum, who apparently was given an overnight lesson on parenting, and Neelo basically told my mother that she was being unfair for not wanting to see me happy, and that just because I was seeing a Muslim woman was not going to make me less of a son to my mother. This must have been the "wake up call" and the last straw because in the next twenty four hours, the entire saga was somewhat reversed. My mother began to cut me and Rose some "slack" and she was beginning to come to terms with our relationship. I really have no idea what had transpired, but if you were to look at my mother and my wife today, they have been described as "a house on fire', and this is in-spite of the fact that we live in different parts of the world. I guess, sometimes, miracles do happen. There are really no answers, just choices.

Now that the external turbulence seemed to be settling down, and life was gaining its momentum on an equilibrium that seemed to stabilize its path, it was time for me to personally overcome the main obstacle - the surgery. Even before the surgery, I had so many faith healers who would visit me and apply me with options towards healing. Eventually, after we would spend countless hours getting rid of them, we left Singapore and headed back home to Johor Bahru. I needed to be in my own home again, but I had a split in my personal opinion and wondered how it should be categorized. I would say that my feelings at the time seemed to be like a tug of war between my 'inner psyches' which created this tension between my higher senses of purpose versus my lower sense of apprehension. Does this make sense? I knew that I was struggling with this purpose and mission at hand, and it became more apparent that this turmoil and struggle was between the wisdom and ignorance of my inner nature.

On a more positive note, dealing with this dilemma started to reveal some true colours that it was an evolutionary drive towards the full realization of my own potential – my inner most human spirit to get over cancer and heal with the passage of time. I wanted to regain my birth right to live, and live with a purpose. If I had to live with cancer, then it needed to be an adventure. There would be no compromises, because that would be admitting failure and I hated that. The war within was between the inertia of my biological heritage and the irrepressible drive to fulfil what was latent in my nature. I knew that surgery was going to result in a lot of pain, although I wasn't sure of its magnitude then. While suffering was a choice that I was not going to make, I knew that without some notion of suffering, there would be no real incentive to heal. We've all heard of the old adage "no pain, no gain"! I looked up some literature on this matter and it was revealed to me in a more spiritual sense in the Bhagavad Gita where it is summarized as follows:-

> *"In every one of us, by virtue of our being human,*
> *there is an upward surge to evolve, to grow in humanity*
> *day by day, and a downward pull to remain engaged in*
> *conflict as separate creatures set against the rest of life"*

I decided that if there was going to be suffering from this surgery, which hadn't even been performed I might add, then I would use it as a larger piece of the healing equation, where I would engage its properties to grow and place some greater emphasis on my apparent state of fear and my own inhibitions. I would express upon myself that it was time to remove myself from all aspects of an internal and save environment that I had created. This seemed to perpetuate some form of a conditioned behaviour and I needed to do something crazy, perhaps audacious but within limits. This was when I came up with the loftiest idea that I would admit myself into Mt. Elizabeth Hospital at least a week before the surgery to acclimatize myself to the surrounding and hospital environment.

I asked for a single room which came with a sofa set, television, bar fridge and a pull out bed. This was like a hotel suite, and while I knew what this was going to cost me per day, I was not in the least bit bothered about it. Insurance would take care of at least eighty five percentage of the cost and I got to stay in a marvellous room and be treated like a king. The day finally drew nearer and on the 2nd of July, 1996, I was admitted into hospital and in an instant, I felt that I was going to get through the ordeal. What had changed? I had no idea then, but it dawned on me a few days later than this room enabled me to entertain my visitors, who had arrived from all over the country, including Malaysia. My two best friends Shanti and Michael were the first to visit, followed by my landlord in Johor Bahru, scores of people from my work group, clients, and not to forget my brother, sister, Ruben, mother, aunts, cousins and a host of relatives, who apparently had figured out that they could practically camp in my room. I was unfazed by all of this simply because I had my people around me, and it made me feel really safe.

The days went by really fast and just three days prior to surgery; I was placed on a low residue diet to enable me to clear my bowels more effectively. This was a truly significant surgery.

I remember it like I was having my first "joint" in university. Just twenty four hours prior to going under the knife, Professor E.C Tan, my urologist gave me another surprise. Not only was I expected to endure a Colostomy, but now, there was a possibility of ending up with a "Urostomy" and that I would never be able to father a child! Once again, the "Oh Shit" feeling consumed me, in its entirety, and I was alone at the time, undergoing the bowel preparation. This news was all too much to fathom and I broke down, this time in silence. The feeling of having failed overpowered my sense of belonging. It stopped me in my tracks and it was about to worry me senseless. What if I didn't make it? What if the thought of having to live with two "bags" would prove too much to endure? What if I would need to have this for the rest of my life?

This feeling of having failed, despite my heroic attempt to undergo vigorous radiation therapy, was about to become a huge phenomenon. I searched for some answers, but there was no reprieve at the time. The only thing that I could do was to examine my life up to the moment, and I started to make some sense of it, amidst the uncertainty. While life, up to the moment, was seen through my eyes as an invisible entity, it needed some continuation before it withered away. I was not about to let it go and surrender to some force that appeared to be gaining in momentum, but rather to summon everything that I had, within me, to feel its presence, its existential relevance, and its way forward. I knew then, that no matter what happens - life will inevitably take on some form of character with its essence intact. Yes, perhaps it would still be driven around like a well- oiled Alfa Romeo.

Although life, in relation to this account, would be seen as a reinvention, aspiring, and inspiring towards a personal transformation, I was also about to decipher its ingredients and it needed to be examined right from the beginning, from its infancy stage. I needed to intensify its significance and in doing so, personify the subconscious mind. You see, I had also realized that my subconscious mind was unable to tell the difference between what I had experienced versus what I had experienced with emotional intensity. I realized that this was still early days in the course of my treatment, on-going battles, and living with a certain element of dignity. This early diagnosis of life was about to define the most powerful and influential part or ingredient that I would apply later on towards maintaining and preserving that much needed and desired sense of reality, that sense of purpose, belonging, and most importantly, a stable state of mind.

In the next few hours throughout the night, I came to terms with my fate, and while there were clearly no answers, there were choices to be made, and I was able to live with these choices, for they were my choices. After sorting out all the questions that were flowing through my mind, I decided to stop worrying and began to listen to the surrounding, to tune in to every sound and alienate them one by one. Just like I used to buy one twenty four hour day, day in and day out, listening to the silence in between allowed me to play with the power of anticipation as it entered my mind.

It was about 3am in the morning and the bowel preparation was almost done. I needed to talk to someone and remember calling my good friend Michael and I discussed what the doctor had said. Michael was engaging, encouraging, and supportive. He listened intently, and then offered me some words of comfort. He said that in the course of his duty as a crew member on board his long flights, he had, on many occasions, attended to passengers who had two "bags"! I was amazed to hear that these passengers were actually able to travel. In an unceremonious swoop, I was going in for a life altering surgery for stage four advanced rectum cancer and I knew then that I was going to kick this in the ass. Instead of thinking about having failed, I began to summon all notions of success and what it meant to me. This was personal, private, and it was all mine to define.

Throughout the remaining hours, I allowed the feeling of success to enter into my mind, allowing it to lodge itself deep within the walls of fear and uncertainty, and all my hopes, thoughts, visions and dreams of living a near normal life after this was beginning to see some light! I reaffirmed a few principles that I had held very close to heart, and in a spirited sense, made one thing clear to my conscious mind - that I was not going to let fear overcome my thoughts of success. I was born with limited fears and everything else that had transpired was due to circumstances. I could reverse them - it was my choice. It had to be done. The moment had arrived, and with everyone close to me being there to support me and urge me on, I was wheeled into surgery. Even under sedation, I could still recognize the nervous anticipation, the excitement, and the near reverence with which my family and loved ones had approached this dreaded moment.

I said my goodbyes to everyone, and told them all that I would be seeing them later in the evening. I remember being informed that the surgery was expected to last eight hours and prepared my family for a 'long haul'. In the waiting area right next to the operating theatre in which Professor Abu Rauff was going to perform his miracle, my uncle was granted access to keep me company, and it was then that I realized something – I had heard my father's voice, calling out to me to say that I was going to be fine. Somehow, throughout the past week, my father had never entered my thoughts until that very day. Uncle Maha and my father were very close, and when the nurse asked me who this man was, standing next to me in the waiting area, I confidently said, "he's my father". Tears were rolling down my cheeks as I was taken into the operating theatre, waving goodbye to my uncle. The nurses and anaesthetist placed great importance on ensuring that I was comfortable before explaining to me about the next step – putting me to sleep. I vaguely remember seeing Professor Abu Rauff and mentioning that he should say a prayer before beginning the operation, to which I heard him say, "We'll all say a prayer"! I closed my eyes............

11

Crossing the Rubicon

"The only way is forward"

I woke up in recovery after what had been an eight hour surgery. I remember one distinct feeling - I was shaking uncontrollably from the cold. There was, however, no pain - I felt nothing, and the lower half of my body felt completely numb. I wasn't able to comprehend this until the theatre nurse attendant mentioned that I was given an epidural to ease the pain. I had no idea what this was until very much later. In any case, besides the trembling and shivering, I appeared to be in good shape as I was wheeled into High Dependency. There, I began to feel thick layers of blankets over me, and it suddenly dawned on me that I wasn't able to feel the "bags" – the 'colostomy and Urostomy'. The colostomy was explained earlier in this journey but a 'Urostomy' was needed as a result of the bladder being invaded by cancer. This meant that my bladder would have been removed and the urinary passage would be diverted out to the walls of my abdomen, to facilitate urinary functions. Doesn't all this sound like a plot from the movie, ET!?

I gestured at the night nurse who was attending to me and asked if there were any bags on me and she said no. NO! REALLY!! NO

SHIT!!! I was elated, but with all the tubes in my mouth and nose, I wasn't able to say anything. I looked around me and all I could see were machines, digits, beeps, pumps, and I wondered why all this seemed to be connected to my body. I had a short panic attack but it disappeared quickly when I saw my brother, sister, mother, and Rose in front of me, grinning like someone had won the lottery. Rajiv came up to me, kissed my hand and said, "No Bags" – nothing. Apparently Professor Abu Rauff managed to pull of one hell of a miracle and in the process, saved my bladder and colon. All I had was a urinary catheter and that was it. I couldn't believe this stroke of good fortune and the feeling of great relief punctuated by tears running down my cheeks was unmentionable. The suave and sophisticated Professor Abu Rauff, whose bedside manners reminded me of a pontificating man, pulled it off, and the prognosis was looking good. How did this happen? I had prepared myself for the worst and ended up discovering this treasure of good fortune!

After a brief encounter with my immediate family and Rose, I remember seeing my uncle Jegadeva, my father's younger brother, who had flown in from Kuala Lumpur to see me. He was always by my mother's side, and would attend to her every wish and demand, and would drop whatever he would be doing if ever my mother called on him. Uncle Jega came in and held my hand and said "we're all very happy for you" and left as it was already getting late. This was past visiting hours, and it was time for me to say good night. I spent the night surrounded by strange and weird sounds of machines, but it somehow wasn't that difficult to handle, and eventually, I must have dozed off into a deep sleep. The feeling of utter relief consumed me because prior to the surgery, my mind was preoccupied with the pain from surgery and the fear that cancer was going to take my life. These fears are the main reasons why so many people would frown upon the

word "cancer". After all, if I were to look back into the fear of pain
and death that cancer had bestowed upon my family, watching
my father suffer, and experiencing first hand, how cancer had
practically reduced him to a skeleton, it seemed that we all had
a trained culture that regarded cancer with horror and treated it
like a negative event.

However, I had summoned the steel in me, and had plenty of
time to digest what was about to transpire, and I kept reminding
myself that if I was going to live with cancer, then it needed
to be an adventure. I was never going to negotiate with this
illness, let alone give it the opportunity to inflict anymore harm
that it already had. Most of all, I was not going to allow it to
drag my family down with unmanageable or negative events.
Whatever was about to happen, it needed to function out of the
boundaries of pain, panic, or undue tension. There needed to be
a fundamental condition in which, I would be able to deal with
pain in self-defence. Fear needed to be eliminated, and not only
from my mind, but from the minds of my immediate family, and
especially my beloved mother. She had already lost her husband to
cancer, and now she was facing the possibility of losing her eldest
son. I was not going to let this happen.

We are all too familiar with the notion of fear and its influence
that extends beyond the patient. It becomes painfully obvious
that relatives and friends become preoccupied with whether
their loved ones are in pain or not. This concern is natural, and
of course reasonable to expect, but as I've said, I've personally
experienced this before, and this undue preoccupation is usually
accentuated and often muddled by the relatives' own personal
fears. To me, this was not healthy, as it could lead to an unnatural
preoccupation and the next thing on the plate would be tension
and anxiety. Why was all this necessary when it would only cause

more problems for the patient's recovery process – my recovery process. I was not in the mood to play host to cancer now, even though I had this magnificent room in the hospital ward.

It was about 5am in the morning, when the nurses came into my cubicle and indicated that they would clean me up and change the sheets. I wondered how they were going to achieve this with me on the bed! This was a really an act of twisting, turning, balancing, and in all these surprising movements, I was given a wipe down, brushed my teeth, had the sheets changed and was all ready for breakfast. Unbelievable!! I was dying of thirst and hunger but I noticed the signage over the bed head which read "nil by mouth". No big deal - I had all the right nutrients being pumped into me intravenously, and it was indicated that it would probably be a good week before I was able to tolerate any food or drink. So it was time to wait for the surgeon to arrive as I was curious about the surgery. Was it successful? Does this mean that I'm now cancer free? There I was, lying in this strange place which appeared to be so sterile and germ free. I had an eight inch incision made on my belly and god knows what else had been done. But this was unforgettably the sweetest moment in my personal life, having endured this, and was still in one piece. I sensed victory, and knew that it was the pinnacle of my state of awareness. This conscious state was no longer dim - I was able to see some light and remembering my brother's expression of unrestrained amazement reinforced the fact that I could have possibly made it. In a small but significant way, I had achieved climbing to the base camp of Mount Everest and viscerally, instinctively and spiritually, there was no turning back. I had crossed the Rubicon.

It was at this moment that I knew that this illness was not going to consume me. I was going to survive this and live poignantly, audaciously as I knew how, and stood firm to the notion that in no time, I would be back in my favourite playground, surrounded by carpets and rugs. Up to this point, I had taken everything in my life for granted, and now, I was overwhelmed with anxiety, victory and an achievable level of success, possibly heading down the road as a cancer survivor. Naturally, being the man I was, thoughts of searching for the crossroads in my life would intermittently invade my recovery, and I would ask many questions as to where it all went wrong. How did I get into this mess so early in my life? Was this all due to the family history or was fate dealing a crucial blow. However strong these interruptions were, I promised myself that I would do everything to manipulate and amuse all the empty spots that were so evidently clear in my life, and vowed to change my ways.

Now that the camouflage had been removed, waking up to the notion that I may have prevailed in my quest to battle this illness left me somewhat naked to my immediate surroundings, shortcomings, vulnerabilities, and inadequacies. No doubt, they all appeared to be clear, and this no longer burdened me with the necessity to appear otherwise. I could just be myself and let time take its course. The doctors and my surgeon dropped in after a while and explained that the surgery went unexpectedly well and that my colon had been reattached after the affected parts had been removed. And to add icing to the cake, the initial diagnosis of bladder cancer was now reversed. While the tumour had spread to the bladder from the rectum, this was benign and to play it safe, a portion of my bladder had been removed. This meant that with the passage of time, the bladder would eventually adjust to its new size and resume all its functions after some much needed rest – I needed to have the catheter in me for a considerable period of time. I suppose this was a "walk in the park" compared to the initial prognosis that I was expected to lose the bladder, have a permanent colostomy, Urostomy, and that I would probably be impotent. For the first time in a long time, destiny had dealt a favourable hand.

After four days in High Dependency, I was moved into the normal ward, and I found myself back in my little kingdom of a luxurious one bedroom suite like enclosure. The family area in this room was conveniently and laboriously detailed with accessories that would come in handy for my family. There was a nice pull out bed, three seater sofa, television, private telephone line, and a bar refrigerator. With all this prevailing, I had no time to think of what this was going to cost me, and conveniently left it to the insurance company. Little did I realize that this very first admission was the onset of what could possibly be categorized as the 'mother of all financial melt-downs'. Now I was the thirty two year old cancer victim, who after having enjoyed a short but successful career, was about to enter into another dimension, where my lifelong fear and aberration of failure had been shoved to the lowest basement level in a multi-storey building!

Cancer had been ruthless to the point that a large portion of the colon and rectum had been removed, bladder excised to 50% of its original size, and the ureter routed to facilitate a near normal urinary function. Cancer was a wake-up call and reminded me that I was not a star or a superhero, and made me feel vulnerable as I often felt that I was going to die, despite having survived my first major surgery in thirty two years of my life. My whole life had been based on the premise that success was inevitable if I worked hard, and that no matter what circumstances would prevail, I was always going to be a star. However, this illness was starting to show its colours, its true force, which up to this point, had dominated and reduced my extended family on my father's side with a very prominent history. This was evidently clear, and in a matter of days after being taken into the normal ward, I had to face up to another challenge, one that meant that my entire life's purpose was somehow a charade and appeared to be completely hypocritical.

As it turned out, the surgery had resulted in an unexplained turn of events, as I soon discovered that there was a communication between the rectum and the bladder walls – there were traces of 'faeces' that seemed to be appearing through the penile entry, a mucus like formation but somehow odourless. Medically known as a "fistula", this abnormal connection between the two organs resulted in unmentionable pain. This was certainly undeniable and the agony was now real. I began to panic in a way that I had never before. This was an intangible moment and in one swift move, Professor Abu Rauff decided to act, and confirmed the prognosis via a CT scan. It was clear that I needed another surgery, barely one week after enduring the first one. Was this all one ridiculous dream? I was so pleased with myself after the first surgery, and had vowed that I was never turning back. Now, I was faced with another dilemma. Why was this happening? Questions, questions, and more questions!

I voiced out my frustration in anger and took it out on the people in my inner circle and I remember my beloved mother having to endure the major part of my outbursts. God forgive me and I hope that my mother would too, as I would ask for some solace while sending out signals during a silent prayer. Most of the time, I kept everything inside, unexpressed, but smouldering with an attendant sense of justice. I wasn't able to comprehend this sudden turn of events, and while I was a person who had never lost perspective of appreciating all that I had achieved so far, this response was understandable, yet illogical! I just felt that I was a victim of random, vindictive fate. I would ask myself over and over again if something as serious as cancer can be attributed to "bad luck"? Very much earlier in this book, I spoke about cause and effect and I realized and acknowledged that the whole universe as we know it, is governed by a set of laws, the principle one being that for every action, there is an equal and opposite reaction. But I asked again and again, if I could be excluded from these laws because at this very moment, I refused to accept the fact that I had cancer as a result of what I had done in the past. This was a situation where I felt so utterly disappointed and damaged beyond repair, and I began to allow all the negative thoughts of an early death consume me - and it all seemed to be beyond my control. Professor Rauff confirmed my worst fear - that I would need a colostomy. This was needed to allow the colon to 'rest' and prevent any trauma from facilitating its normal functions later on. I asked what this meant and The Professor mentioned that this was going to be a temporary colostomy; I would need to endure it for approximately three months before it could be reversed. As I grew to see myself as a combination of things, and a recipient of many blessings, I simply could not accept this and I wasn't prepared for this, not after having escaped it the first time. However, there was no time to waste, since the fistula was already causing some serious infection, not to mention the unbearable pain.

I was wheeled into surgery for the second time, and I remember being so angry at my surgeon - I felt that he had deceived me. As I was being prepared for surgery, I recalled my younger days, and acknowledged that while I may have been a narcissistic and ruthless lad in my early twenties, I certainly didn't deserve this. I had no education on this course of action, and I wasn't able to conjure up the image of having a colostomy, despite having read some literature on it and watched a video on the subject matter. I was a man who enjoyed partying and I wondered if I would be able to dance again - would I be able to make love with a colostomy and how was I able to deal with 'faeces' coming out on to my body in a bag!!! I thought to myself, just before surgery, that this would be a really good day to die.

As a young man with sensualist inclinations, this was a perfect getaway. As I was taken into the operating theatre, my surgeon came up to me and said, "We are all already saying a prayer" so don't worry, you're going to be fine. Easy for him to say, he wasn't about to endure this surgery? I knew that I was responsible for feeling like a victim because I had allowed all these negative thoughts to enter my mind. Strangely, I was able to indulge in these emotions and felt sorry for myself. But at this moment, I was alone, by myself, and on the operating table, ready to be put to sleep. The feeling of helplessness all seemed to be justifiable, and I felt that despite the prognosis up to that moment - I had no part in the development of the illness. Still, the situation now was all too surreal, and I had a brief moment to look into my premeditated pattern of behaviour. I felt that I needed some defence mechanism to cope with this situation instead of feeling like a victim of cancer.

I searched deep within me and found a very small element of hope which I had been clinging on to, and I decided then and there that I would seek this sense of hope to manage the situation at hand. I needed to have my life back, and if it meant that it was going to be with a temporary colostomy, then so be it. I don't know what had changed in such a very brief moment, but I began to see my life as being tolerable again. Instead of trying to please everyone with an overtone of passive subservience, it was time to please myself, and that meant that I would no longer see myself as a victim, but more of a patient. As a patient, this meant that I would recover with the right treatment, and by showing some patience; this would perhaps lead to a calmer endurance of any given situation, stressful or otherwise. This also meant that I would be able to persevere in a more relentless way and began to see myself as a normal human being, living comfortably with a colostomy. The notion of no longer being a victim of cancer was starting to look like a damn good and fine attribute and I summoned the steel in me again. I remembered the exhilaration that I had felt when I had crossed the Rubicon the first time and I wanted that sense of achievement again.

The anaesthetist came up to me and adjusted my arm to insert the needle in and began the process of "knocking me out". My favourite phrase then was "hammer time" – don't ask! I suddenly felt excited at the prospect of living again and I knew that after this surgery, I would be able to function normally and I would train my mind to broaden the horizons and take account of the full spectrum of possibilities to understand my illness better. As I was about to "go under", I was able to see some possibility of exploring the physical, emotional, mental, and spiritual realms of my existence, and began to fathom a healing environment. I knew it was not going to be easy, but the only way was forward......

There was a burning sensation in my arm as I went into a deep sleep............

12

The Recovery

"Action is not conscious, it's compulsive"

It must have been at least four hours since the surgery, and waking up in the recovery room greeted me with intense anxiety and pain. This time there was no epidural and I was practically screaming in agony. I remember asking the operating theatre nurse if any pain medication had been administered. I felt like my insides had been gutted, and all I wanted to do was to rip out all the tubes and run. The nurses were patient with me, and tried to calm me down, while they topped up the pain medication. I had another epiphany, as I felt the colostomy bag on the right hand side of my lower abdomen. It felt warm and weird – the pain was something else. I wondered why it was as intense as my unestablished mind was playing tricks with my thought process. I felt like this was an unnecessary moment. I wanted this unsettling feeling to go away then and there, but it was not meant to be. I was imitating a sense of acceptance to try to reduce the intensity of my thought process, but the thought of having to live with this alien object on my body was beginning to manifest itself as something too far-fetched.

I was terrified to say the least. After what must have felt like an eternity, I was moved to the ward and my family and colleagues from work were already waiting for me in the room. I settled into my bed and then it was all quiet, as I remember really struggling with the colostomy. I had wished for everything else but this, and I remember telling myself that if everything that I had wished for became a reality, then I would be in trouble, so perhaps this was a blessing in disguise! You see, I was an absolute mess and nothing was making sense. The only consolation was that this was a temporary colostomy and in a matter of time, I would be able to gain my freedom back.

Professor Abu Rauff came in to see me after the surgery and mentioned that the procedure went according to plan, and that the colon would need to rest for at least three months, after which, I would need another assessment to ensure that the fistula was no longer an issue. In the interim, I needed to have the urinary catheter in me throughout the three month period in order to give the bladder some time to heal as well. This seemed pre-ordained as I saw it, but it was not an easy task to handle. I would have a colostomy and an external urine bag. I called it my Louis Vuitton! I needed to inject some humour into this episode while recovering in hospital. The following days were consumed with insurmountable pain and anxiety, and dealing with the colostomy resulted in a couple of mishaps.

I remember one particular evening when the bag burst open, spilling out all the bodily waste that had been accumulating over the period of the day. It was awful and the stench that was being emitted made be even more ill. I had to deal with it, and it became painfully obvious that the only remedy was for me to ignore the fact that I had a colostomy. It needed to be treated as part of my body, my anatomy and my well-being. I began to accept this strange object which looked like an unusually large floatation device that would fill up even when I would have sips of water. Over a short period, my body began to function normally, and I was allowed to eat in very small doses. I was able to manage and in just a matter of days, I began to walk again. This sense of freedom was overwhelming but what was not improving was the pain.

The plan after surgery would include a radical course of chemotherapy. This was fluorouracil (5-FU), specially designed for the treatment of colon cancer, and I was expected to endure at least eight sessions over a period of six months. However, I had another serious issue at hand, the intensity of relentless pain that just refused to ease up. After repeated scans, the surgeons finally decided to put me on Pethidine, the wonder drug. This post-operative drug did its job and the pain was slowly but surely controlled. Besides pain relief, this drug would give me temporary euphoric highs along with a sense of peace and serenity, often bordering on mindless hallucinations. It was at this time that I was warned about pethidine addiction. To assist in writing more convincingly about this matter, I did some research into pethidine addiction and apparently this can strike at random, and no one in their right mind would take pain killers with the intention of getting 'hooked', and that it was purely administered for pain relief.

However, this was not in my case, as I soon began to display all the behavioural traits of an addict. I ignored all the warning signs which were clearly being demonstrated in fine fashion such as severe mood swings, drowsiness, chest pains, tremors, low blood pressure, and the list goes on. I loved the "buzz" it gave me, although short lived, but the chemically induced sensation from the drug was just too good to refuse. As expected, the highs were so transient that I would orchestrate instances to get more injections by intensifying the pain level in my system. I even managed to convince the doctors that I needed greater and more frequent doses in order to stabilize the pain that I was experiencing. My body was so 'in tune' with pethidine that when the doctors tried to administer every second dose with a placebo effect, which was normal saline through the injections, I would be able to recognize it immediately. You must understand that this was a period when I was looking for ways and means to die; I wanted an early death even though I had created this whole scenario of having accepted my state of being. To access this state of being, I regarded it as an analysis of my existence, my human existence, transcending beyond my character into unchartered waters. I looked at it as a form of a unique language beyond what some philosophers would describe as "metaphysical".

I needed to examine my fascination for all things that appeared to be timeless, in a sense that I viewed the feeling of euphoric highs as being intensely timeless. It would transport me to another dimension and pain would no longer be an issue, but more of a phenomenon. Even in a drowsy state, I was still able to ask myself if this state of being existed in reality, or was it already an existing condition - that is to say if this was to be expected. My brother Rajiv introduced the teachings of Martin Heidegger to me, and mentioned ever so eloquently in the introduction to this book that, like his teachings, my journey gathers rather than collects - as a commitment to further explaining the concept of different meanings together. Heidegger goes on to mention that the study of Ontology will further clarify this thought process. Here, he says that, *"ontology in analytical philosophy, concerns the determination whether some categories of being are fundamental and asks in what sense the items in those categories can be said to be"*

The constant dependency on 'Pethidine' personified the sense of pain management as I knew it to be, a simple phenomenon, which was like a science of consciousness. Understanding its function was as fundamental as its identity itself. The phenomenological reduction helped me to free myself from the prejudice of being labelled as an addict, and gave me the innate sense that I was merely observing my behaviour and actions. In this context, my actions were toxic and compulsive, and I was able to encounter all the negative aspects of being dependent on this wonder drug. I was an independent observer. I saw it as a method, somewhat justifiable, in dealing with the pain.

Over time, the management of the pain started to improve, and the plan was to gradually reduce the dosage so that I could go home. The thought of returning home was thrilling and exciting, yet I was faced with anxiety as I wasn't ready to give up the injections. My body had adjusted to the presence of this drug, and would compensate for it and as time progressed, resistance to the drug was rapidly formed. In short, my mind would re-compensate, and the need for more 'pethidine' was firmly established as a pattern. I tried to negotiate with everyone - my family, nurses, doctors, Rose, as no one could see the logic in my trying to drug myself to an early death. However, in order to stabilize my body, I wasn't ready to give in to the reduction in dosage just yet. I would have countless hours of intense pain, more like withdrawal symptoms when the drug was not administered on time. My surgeon, having realized that a slow period of adjustment would probably be best, decided that the hospitalization would continue for a few more days to monitor the situation. I had managed to create an internal state of ethos, and the philosophy of getting over the pain from cancer and two surgeries was simply to "get more pethidine"! Over the next few days, the consequences were exponential; I would have episodes of ridiculous hallucinations and epileptic seizures. Naturally, no one was impressed and to say that they were worried would be an understatement.

This was also beginning to worry me senseless, even though I was also quietly basking in the glory of receiving my regular "fix" every four hours. In the course of the following days, I began to recall the many people whom I had read about, whose fight with cancer seemed to be much more dignified. I was able to tell what all these people must have felt. On one hand, the energy and excitement that had been created as a result of winning must have given them hope, and this seemed to create the buoyancy that I needed. It showed me that this victory could very well be magical, if I were to put my heart and soul into a much more formidable healing process. However, on a much deeper level, I also came to a realization that I was also the repository of that hope and have been, at some point, privy to it, while recognizing that it now had a life of its own, a kindled spirit, which seemed to transcend beyond my control.

In order to restore that sense of hope and balance out the feelings that I was experiencing, I needed to capture it, restore some faith in it, and tame its fierce outrage. I realized that this was an independent entity with my psyche, and as much as I was battling a debilitating illness, I also had to reconcile with everyone's expectations, that I was going to pull through. Let's face it, unless one had actually experienced what I was going through, it was impossible for them to know what I was feeling, therefore I needed to plot this recovery out carefully, knowing full well that all the high expectations couldn't possibly be met in its entirety. Well that's what I was telling everyone - this was a difficult battle, while realizing that my personal spirit shouldn't be too restrained.

When it finally dawned on me that if this spirit in me were to depart, the people spurring me on, my family and loved ones, would be left with another sense of reality. This was something that I had never denied, that cancer was going to take my life away at such an early age, and I kept bringing this to everyone's attention. I would ask my doctor how much time I had left and usually never received a straight answer. I became more confused and disillusioned in the process, and entered into a deeper dimension of pain, self-inflicted perhaps, but it was real.

All this was just too real to ignore. In between the near death experiences that I had encountered on numerous lonely nights, it was understandable that my inner circle of friends and family decided that they would step in and lead the way in ensuring that I would not give up, and with their help and persistence, we became an unstoppable and formidable force. I could not help but feel that this force was a deception on our respective parts, certainly not done deliberately, but resulted or accumulated due to the sheer will. All the hard choices that were ahead of me could somehow be dealt with. Perhaps, this was a delusional factor in my quest to battle this illness, while resting on the fact that, I seemed to be in a safe haven, since the pain was now no longer an issue. The days ahead needed to be better, the dependency and addiction towards drugs needed to be eliminated, and with a great force beckoning my sense of achievement, the rekindled spirit took over all the negative feelings that appeared to be in the air.

The audacious thing I needed to do was to get back on my feet as fast as possible and get back to work. I searched for the fire in me, within me, and summoned the nerve to be more effective in dealing with the pain. I needed an extraordinary approach to be more disciplined. The feeling of allowing this illness to take over my life was running amok in my daily life, so it was time to rally my troops, and be imperturbable. There was a voice in me that kept reminding me of the good life that I had enjoyed prior to being diagnosed, and I desperately wanted that life back. I would sit back in bed and imagine being on a beach in Bali or walking down the shores of Lombok with Rose, while sipping on my favourite cocktail. It was a rare moment of a self-fulfilling prophecy and it all suddenly appeared to be more achievable and realistic. I suppose the inner team had been assembled, my inner most spirit had been re-born, and I needed to be that tenacious fighter once again, while synthesizing the external factors like my mood swings, and feelings of rage, and anger.

There was nothing more to analyse now, or to explain or predict. It was time to get up, and get out of hospital. I can tell you that the single driving force behind my recovery, in its initial stages, was my mother, who played a role that no one else could have, and the love she had for her son could not be explained any more than it was always painfully obvious. My mother's strategy was her believe in a higher power, one that would save me with her constant prayers, chanting of versus from Sai Baba's songs, and just being there for me, day and night - would be the beginning of a critical but important point in my recovery.

I was entering a poignant moment where it was evidently clear that a radical change was necessary. There were times when I felt that my brain had finally become scrambled, and I would have to come to terms that incapacity wasn't far off the charts. It was quickly revealed to me in a quiet moment one morning, that there must be a prevailing condition in which we, as human beings, would strive to enter in to a new dimension of discovery, for the purpose of attaining the optimum level of some form of personal satisfaction. This meant that the "modus operandi" would inevitably manipulate all aspects of self- gratification in the paradox of living and recovering under any circumstances. The optimum level of personal satisfaction meant that I would come to terms with living with a temporary colostomy. I summoned every effort to get out of hospital, reduce my dependency on drugs, and started a process of looking ahead and moving forward. This course of action needed to be compulsive, and justifiably non-negotiable. I had to be really hard on myself, and enter into a new territory of living, and it began with an education. This was a revelation into the dangers of extreme drug dependency. I needed to look for a way forward and establish a permanent commitment to a certain way of life, and there would be no "turning back".

However, I was still in a state of deep emotional stress and physical discomfort, so it was suggested that I take "baby steps", which simply meant that I would need to get out of this 'mode' by employing a slow but steady and consistent method of recovery. I had absolutely no idea where to start, but if you've been following my thought process so far, you would have figured out that I was quite capable of coming up with great and lofty ideas in order to prevail, just quietly…….

Over the next few days, scores of visitors came to see me, and commented on how good I looked. I needed this re-assurance, and I remember one morning when old man Mr Hassan from the Company had stopped by on his way back from the bank, his usual morning route. It was a quiet morning, and he sat next to me on the chair and said "I can't believe how much weight you've lost", and I noticed tears in his eyes. This was the most resilient of men that I have ever encountered in my career to date, and to see him in this light woke me up. He made it known that I was needed back at work, not for anything else, but to be with the family again. This was a bit like a love affair with the work place, and I knew that I was being looked after here, always and with no conditions attached. My relationship with everyone at work and with the establishment allowed me to appreciate the sense of being valued, and like a newly formed union, I would envisage myself growing old with everyone - learning all the "ropes" together, arguing and going against each other at times, but always yearning and striving to retain the profundity in our relationship, which to me, meant everything. I never looked at the possibility of this relationship breaking up, it was always meant to be, I thought!

As the week was coming to an end, my doctors came in to deliver some much needed good news. I was on a steady course of recovery, and the infection was settling nicely. My bowel movements had somewhat been restored and regulated to include the functions of a colostomy, and my bladder was healing. I would need to have the urine catheter in for a few more weeks, and then it would be removed. I was thrilled to say the least, and practically jumped out of bed to greet this positive turn of event. After the usual internal assessments, I was issued my discharge papers and the bill, of course, which I remember amounted to Singapore – currency $31,000. I had no 'Medisave' (government assisted medical insurance) or CPF (central provident funds), that was sufficient to cover this cost, but I was insured privately. Without any hesitation, I pulled out my gold American Express and paid the bill. My immediate family and Rose had chipped in with a very generous and sizeable donation towards my expenses, and I was all set to go home.

My mother, who had been waiting for this day, was excited, cautious, worried, and thrilled to say the least, because her eldest son was coming home. We were still staying in Johor Bahru, in Bukit Kempas, with the rest of the family, and we had Chivas, my brother's German Sheppard, whose pedigree name was Riverbanks Henry II. Chivas was a great companion, but a rather difficult dog to manage, and train, definitely due to our lack of training skills, and our own inhibitions of learning how to cope and manage with a thoroughbred animal. Nevertheless, this dog had arrived at the most opportune moment, as I would yearn to have him in my company over the course of my recovery at home. Coming home after surgery had its moments, but it also revealed that I was able to heal with an extraordinary sense of possibility. I was at home now, in my own kingdom, and there were no injections, no machines hooked up to me, and no interruptions, when I retired to bed every night. Having my mother, sister, and family re-assured my commitment towards the task at hand - I would need to recover quickly. Rose and I had shared the purchase of a car, a Peugeot 405, which I called the beast. I loved this machine and with her by my side, I soon found myself driving again. The urine catheter (Louis Vuitton) bag was now replaced with a smaller and more manageable version which I would attach to my knee, so this meant that I was able to ambulate with relative ease. From here on, I never lost sight of the mission at hand, my optimism, self believe, despite the numerous episodes of pain and discomfort. There was an incredible release of energy, and as the weeks went by, the time had come for me to enter into a new phase of recovery.

Rose and I decided that we would take a trip together. Even though we weren't married then, my mother and family had come to see Rose as a member of our family, and as the woman that I was in love with. Their commitment towards accepting her and welcoming her into the family meant a great deal to me, and personally reinforced my sense of purpose. I knew that being complacent about this relationship was a definite "no-no", so I guarded it with respect, and our time together gave us the opportunity to drive our union forward, unrestrained but with a sense of recognition. My actions now were immediate, necessary, and most definitely compulsive, and this was the only approach which I had summoned to appear before me and my family.

Eventually, the day came when I went in to the hospital and received a very good assessment of the prognosis. Yes, the urine catheter was finally removed, and freedom was once again within grasp. The first few hours thereafter were agonizing, but it was a much needed and welcoming breather. My rational side revealed to me that the worse was over, and with a temporary colostomy becoming easier to manage, Rose and I decided to confirm our flight for Lombok, Indonesia. I had never heard of Lombok, but my sister and Ruben had already visited the island which was a forty five minute catamaran ride from Bali. It was also accessible by a direct flight from Singapore, so without any hesitation, Rose and I were all set to go.

So here I was, just eight weeks after two major surgeries, embarking on this trip and all I could think about was the colostomy. I was so afraid that something would happen along the way, and I refused to eat anything prior to the trip. One thing was obvious, although some may look at it as being silly or mundane - the key factor in my journey forward was how I was going to manage my time and the colostomy. The rest would fall into place naturally, but the cardinal importance was time management. I wasn't about to enter into a phase of just lying around doing nothing, or sleeping the whole day, or even worrying myself senseless that I was going to die. No, I needed an adventure, and this was a commitment that I had already made to myself at the beginning, that if I was going to live with cancer, my life needed to function on a different and audacious platform. There would be no negotiations with pain or discomfort as I was prepared to 'suck in all in'!

My schedule in the coming days and weeks needed to be based around certain decisions that would inevitably define my condition. This was clearly an existing condition, and anything routine or formal would only be the ones that were absolutely imperative. Everything else needed to wait! This schedule of mine needed to be a sacred task, and I was the one in charge, The 'CEO' perhaps. No task would appear to be tedious or difficult, as long as I employed sheer vigilance and resilience. Saying "NO" was not an option. The adrenaline rush was clearly apparent, and I had weapons of destruction on stand-by, a will power to push ahead, lofty sense of purpose to achieve the impossible, and a somewhat frightening thought that even though something bad could happen to me on this trip, it needed to happen. I would think, totter, and plot a scheme which meant only one thing - I was going to equip myself with the right attitude, a camera, sufficient amount of cash, and board that flight.

On one Thursday morning, Rose and I boarded Silk Air for Lombok and waved goodbye to our families and loved ones. A conscious and compulsive decision had been made, and it was one of many that I would make in the days and months ahead. At moments like these, in a vault of uncertainty, there is an almost irresistible desire to prevail, and to move forward. There would be instances of fewer pauses, while imploring the circumstances within to gather some signs of support, a sign of victory, and let all negative notions of not being able to live a near normal life dissolve.

This was the beginning of my real recovery…..

13

Setting the tone

"In quiet intensity, I pondered upon the need to expand infinitely"

This holiday was seen as a breakthrough in which, all boundaries that I had built around me were now being removed in pieces. Rose and I walked around the duty free lounge before boarding, and decided to do our fair share of shopping. We picked up two beautiful time pieces, a Longines for her and a Tag Heuer for me. This may have been an impulsive decision but it felt right. An hour later, we were on board the plane, all set for Lombok. We were both excited and apprehensive at the same time, wondering how I was going to handle the journey after surgery, but in the words of Theodore Roosevelt;

> *"It is not the critic, who counts, nor the man who points out how strong man stumbles or where the doer of deeds could have done them better. The credit belongs to the man who is actually in the arena, whose face is marred by dust, sweat and blood, who strives valiantly, who errs, who comes short again and again, because there is no effort without error and shortcomings, but who does actually*

*strive to do the deeds, who knows great enthusiasms, the
great devotion, who spends himself in a worthy cause, who
at best knows in the end that triumph of high achievement,
and who at the worst, if he fails, at least fails while daring
greatly, so that his place shall never be with those cold and
timid souls who neither know victory or defeat"*

In other words, this journey was about getting it done and
conquering my fear of living with cancer and living with a
colostomy. I insisted on one thing, that life should either be a
daring adventure or nothing, because security in any sense did not
exist in nature, nor do the children of men as a whole experience
it. Avoiding danger of any kind, in whatever magnitude, and on
any level, was no safer in the long run than exposure. I was ready
to expose myself as a means to living, and conquer the fear that
was prevailing and embedded deep within my psyche. The first
step was for me to be honest with myself, because I knew that the
process of healing would never progress beyond its initial stage
if I was not going to state the obvious. This was not the time to
digress, instead, this was the time for me to open my eyes and
see the world, pay attention to detail, and to empower myself
and my thought process. Travelling was a means to an end, but
a promising end, in which I was able to heal through people and
their environment. The indigenous culture of the inhabitants
in Lombok revealed a whole new world to me. It was as if they
were still living in a state that I was not accustomed to. However,
understanding the nature of these people and the intensity in their
life helped me to channel pain and come to terms with whatever
turmoil that I was experiencing. I told myself that this was not the
time to feel helpless or disoriented, but to get up and get things
done, to go out and experience the world through the eyes of
the people, who were ever so willing to share their stories, and
experience with me in a clear and structured manner.

Rose and I spent the rest of evening planning our route for the days ahead, and decided that we would visit places of interest, and mingle mainly with the local population, not forgetting shopping for teak furniture. Before I retired for the night, I gathered my thoughts and came to a realization that being in this beautiful resort was somewhat like a sensory perception, in which my personal body, mind and soul, had a presence of its own. I felt a sense of inclusivity, of belonging to the environment, both internally and externally, and it was clear that this experience was boundless. I acknowledged the presence of anxiety and some levels of uncertainty, mainly due to thoughts of having to move around freely with some minor inhibitions, but I felt free and for the first time in a long time, and I knew that this was the life that I wanted. I longed to be able to be free from the clutches of medication and strong opioids, and strived for an expansion of the mind towards an infinite point. However, this meant that I was now able to expand, be it in the moment, or outside the realm of my physical existence, towards a state of connecting with all the elements that were apparent and prevalent in my state of being. This was a means of healing that I needed to equip myself with, and it needed to function as a vehicle to tackle my emotions. This connection allowed me to move through the various channels of my stages of living with my illness, and in a positive way, allowed my mind and body to transgress, to explore possibilities of an endless state of self-fulfilment, and create an extraordinary platform of living, audaciously I might add.

We woke up to a glorious morning, the rays of the morning sun peeking through the shades in our room. After a round of much needed coffee, we headed for breakfast, and paced through the next hour with multiple helpings of local and international cuisine. After breakfast, we walked out to the entrance of the resort and noticed scores of local tour guides who had parked their vehicles, a seven seater range rover or a "kijang" as it's known in the local language, rather prominently. After negotiating a package deal with one of the guides, we signed up for a car and driver, who agreed to spend the rest of the week with us, taking us from place to place.

First on the agenda was the "Sasak" Village, a three hundred year old residential dwelling with structures made from clay and thatched roofing. We were amazed at the sheer brilliance of this structure which had stood the test of time, and with people who had made this place their home and raised a few more generations during their time. Most of the inhabitants were almost seventy to eighty years of age, but they looked incredibly young and fit. We spent the first half of the morning mingling with these people who told us stories of their past and their religion which was Islam. An interesting point to note is that during their time, they would only pray three times a day or as they would categorize as *"Islam Waktu Tiga" (In Indonesian)* I must say that this community had a great impact on me. On the one hand, I knew that my illness was consuming me gradually, but when I looked at the harsh life and conditions in which the local community and their children were living in, this set a tone for a much needed spiritual expansion.

Rose and I standing in front of a 300 year old Sasak dwelling

Up to now, I had experienced pain on a remote level - I had tucked it away and only dealt with it when it became insurmountable, but when I found myself in this remarkable village of people who were living in a cottage like environment, whatever pain that I was experiencing became a mere concept, and it kind of gravitated towards more positive energy. I felt energized, and wanted to connect more with the local people. I found that appreciating and talking to the elders in all aspects of their livelihood represented the immense spirit that was embodied in their existence, and the human resilience was infectious. No matter how remote their physical surrounding appeared to be, I saw so much of creativity, and this made me realize how historically significant their existence meant to them, and this was far more than a shared ideology. Looking back at my life, I was not artistically talented, but I was inclined in this direction to experience my dilemma with my illness, through my own eyes, and with this precious connection that I had made with the local community. In a strange but comprehensible way, it allowed me to be more determined, and gave me the strength to move on and complete my journey.

Appreciating the culture and the people of this Sasak Community related to a higher level of expression. This community was also into weaving beautiful shawls and intricate wall hangings which were made from natural fibres. It allowed me to engage in a dialogue with the weavers, much like the weavers who made rugs on a deeper and more meaningful dimension, and there was an immediate connection between the art form and its creators. To think that all this incredible work was created under such hostile and harsh living conditions was a remarkable discovery. Besides weaving, this community was also responsible for a wide repertoire of wooden carvings, and the reproduction of old and collectible furniture. This was a revelation for us, for we decided to purchase a considerable amount of items for ourselves, and this would serve as our household furniture and decorative compliments when we would eventually purchase our own home one day.

It was time to break for lunch, and we settled in nicely into a local restaurant serving Indonesian food. This was the first time that I had ventured into spicy food after surgery and needless to say, the colostomy was serving its purpose. During lunch, I asked Rose if Cancer was the best thing that happened to me! Perhaps it was, like a wake- up call, but no one in their right mind would have ever wished anything like this onto themselves, or to their enemies. I realized perhaps, that all the stress that I had endured in my life, self-inflicted nonetheless, may have been a contributing factor, over and above the family history. However, from whatever self-discovery towards healing that I had employed to this point, I made it known to myself that being able to appreciate my life, on any level, gave me the power to heal, to cure my mind, and move forward towards a state of acceptance.

This level of honesty was refreshing and encouraging, and as I took baby steps to heal, I refused to be the victim. Instead, I decided to take control. I needed to identify with pain as a form of recovery, to set the pace and tone towards a degree of self-fulfilment, and bravely attempt to do things differently. Pain had the power to consume, and I had to deal with it daily in my quest to be daringly different. In quiet moments, I would yearn for some recognition, both personally and collectively. This trip was seen as a platform in which I would do battle, which involved a plethora of consequences, while understanding its relentless force that would test my endurance and resilience every so often. I was thankful that despite all adversity, I was able to function, and I had Rose with me to help me get through the day, and spur me on to take the challenges that I needed.

After lunch, we ventured into a few art galleries and spent the afternoon looking at paintings by various artists. The paintings were remarkable and breathtakingly beautiful. One would feel that one was transported to heaven and back, when one were to immerse oneself in the kaleidoscope of colours, set against a background of intensity and spatial dimension. As the day progressed, I wanted to soak in some scenes of Lombok, and we asked the driver to take us along the scenic route, where we covered the plains and highlands of Lombok, almost taking us back into another life, another dimension. It was amazing to say the least - so much of nature had been preserved, and the life stock would roam freely within the boundaries that were created by the local inhabitants. It was getting late in the evening, and after a full filled day; it was time for us to return to our little villa by the sea. We made our way to our room and made plans with the driver to meet us again the next morning. After a short rest, Rose and I decided that we would try the buffet dinner in the resort, and we thoroughly enjoyed every moment of it. I mentioned to Rose that I wanted to write about our journey and document all the photos during our trip.

**In my favourite spot – our cosy little
villa by the beach in Lombok**

Later that night, I decided to write about my day and what I had experienced, while Rose took the opportunity to do a spot of reading and retired early. It those days, there were no smart phones, and we actually had more time to converse and connect with each other, without interruptions on our '*viber*' and '*WhatsApp*' applications that we all seem to have today. I made some notes and acknowledged this deep seated desire to succeed, and felt like I needed to be invincible, and to achieve some level of fulfilment on a mammoth scale. This audacious act of bravery came with its persistent bouts of failure and despair. I would mirror my emotional state of mind, and saw for myself that there was an urgent need to change the scenery, and chart a new course in my journey of life. Up to the moment, and reflecting back on my career, I knew that there was a leader in me, waiting to erupt. What better way than to write something about leadership as I saw this as a stepping stone towards a state of recovery.

There are many theories on leadership, but I believe that the core value has to be altruism. While true altruism can sometimes be a myth, it can also be viewed as a transition, often described as personal gratification. While social and other factors affect our consciousness, the burning desire to lead, and be successful, and to prevail against all odds, is a definite possibility. To look at it in a simple yet effective way, we all need to step up and do more, and talk less. I needed to do this more than anything else. The virtues of selflessness need not be examined, or be placed under scrutiny simply because we are all born with an innate gift to lead and succeed. I personally felt that in order to overcome my illness, I needed to lead at the forefront again, and take control. In business, some economic leadership would be fundamentally important, when we are sometimes faced with a situation where we may need to make a deal with the devil and in doing so; this is still a step in the right direction. In terms of understanding prevailing circumstances that might spur on some form of growth or recovery, we need to look at the concept of interiority which is definitely worth exploring, while creating the need to be flexible in our daily quest to lead and succeed. In my view, I only knew the world the way it is projected within me. As it was approaching midnight, I decided to put the pen down and retired for the day.....

Day Two in Lombok greeted us with yet another glorious morning, and after breakfast, it was time to 'hit the trails' of this amazing country. We decided that the day will be filled with shopping for furniture, and to visit some local temples and places of worship. At the foot of the hill on which our resort was located, was an ancestral shrine dating back two hundred years. We had to park by the side of the road of Senaru Village and walk up a steep hill, while taking in the sights of flora and fauna. I stopped in my tracks for a moment while contemplating this climb, because it had been a while since I had attempted anything strenuous like this. However, I was determined to push on, as I was informed of this beautiful waterfall that was at the end of the shrine.

I wondered what the fear was all about, for it was a known fact, well at least in my books, that fear is irrational, and more of a primal instinct, and definitely not a function of a higher brain faculty. Therefore if I were to logically think this through, there was nothing to be afraid off. Somehow, I was petrified, my knees were giving way, and I couldn't bring myself to make this climb. I began to frame my thoughts clearly, and decided that I wasn't about to compromise on my integrity - I needed to be brave and courageous. Rose kept telling me that there was no urgency to do this, but I was adamant and stubborn to say the least. After some much needed internal intervention into my ego, I took the first step, and each step grew more and more certain in its stride, and before long, I was already half way up the trail. I managed to reclaim my pride, and kept telling myself that I am the captain of my own destiny, and I was not about to be governed by fear. To regret later would have been such a waste of precious time.

"Angels whisper to a man when he goes for a walk".

So here I was, about to reach what was probably the most "jaw dropping" waterfall – This was The Sendang Gile waterfall. Located about 600m above sea level, Sendang Gile was also described as The Mt. Rinjani National Park's best known attraction, which welcomed visitors from all over the globe. At the foot of the trail, Rose and I started off at Senaru Village, which housed the ancestral shrine that was apparently the main access to Mt. Rinjani National Park. We climbed over rocks through the tropical forest, and I remember being immensely rewarded by the sheer beauty in nature. When we ascended down the slopes, to reach the waterfall which was an approximately two hundred meter drop, our guide mentioned that the waterfall was also known to have some curative qualities. Needless to say, this was tempting, but since I was already moving around with a colostomy, I wasn't really prepared for this bout of adventure. Nevertheless, we did venture into the water knee deep, and it was just magical.

This was a quiet moment of reflection personally, as I began to envision myself as a barrier breaker. Being in the water and listening to the silence, amidst its surroundings, enabled me to disengage from the pressures of the moment, as my colostomy was already filling up, and it was uncomfortable. However, I paid little attention to it, as I soaked in the brilliance of the immediate surroundings, and recognized the demands that I had placed upon myself, and from the hustle and bustle of the city life that I had left behind. Here, the awesome space and the treasured moment in time enabled me to focus on the challenges that I was about to encounter, and somehow, whatever renewed approaches that I had envisioned in my quest to live extraordinarily, and audaciously with cancer, began to be clearly defined, with a renewed sense of clarity and hope.

There was an inner voice that was giving me the answers. This wasn't some form of isolation, but more of enjoying the moment of solitude with Rose by my side, and it expressed a feeling of completeness and utter fulfilment. All my problems felt distant and unrelated. I mentioned earlier, that life needed to be an adventure, and my journey towards recovery had to be boundless. It was apparent that the recipe for strength was an action plan, and this was an absolute necessity. To put it in simple terms, it meant that no matter how, I was able to achieve a sense of purpose. It was further exemplified by not taking anything for granted, but more of appreciating the simple pleasures of achievement which, by now, appeared to be more productive, joyous, energizing, and essential to my sense of purpose, to my intentions of ascending new heights with no limits. I realized that this was going to be a long haul, but now, I wasn't operating with a "bucket list" attached to my consciousness, but more of having a burning desire to try something new, even if it meant that I was going to break a few rules.

Rose in her comfort zone

The light at the end of the tunnel was clearer now, and in an attempt to cure and heal myself internally and externally, I needed to use solitude, to enhance a sense of creativity from within. This would liberate my mind, and I was able to project this outward, to move forward, and slowly accelerate the pace when I was able to. Fear was no longer something that I felt anymore, perhaps due to the fact that I was willing to expand infinitely, and used creativity in my mind to fuel my growth process. To me, this sense or notion of creativity was the clear voice heard in silence. Before long, it was time for us to head back to the village. After taking some awesome photographs, I realized something and shared this with myself- the cure for my own grief was motion, while the strategy to remain resilient was a form of adventure.

This action was something that I acknowledged, and I was certainly capable of achieving it. I made myself a promise that I would continue to expand and grow towards an infinite level, while refusing to give in to the onslaught of my illness. The million dollar question that I asked myself was; "what was the single force that would control the quality of my life"? The answer was the power of choice. This was the beginning of a new chapter, and it involved a serious commitment to decision making. The irony of it all was that I found the quiet moment that I was desperately searching, in a surrounding that was quite unlike anything that I was accustomed to. Consequently, Rose and I realized that this was an adventure that we were certainly capable of achieving, and it was then that we decided that we would take every opportunity to experience and travel the world together.

We envisioned creative moments creeping into our daily routine, and this would mean that escaping from the clutches of a routine life would have a direct impact on my recovery plan. We were not financially well off at this point, so we knew that we were operating within certain limits to achieve the growth plan. However, this also meant that our surroundings needed to be arranged intelligently, and in such a way that it would stimulate and support our aspirations.

We 'wrapped up' the day with a visit to a few antique furniture shops and saw first-hand, how old and colonial inspired furniture were being re produced. Rose and I took an immediate liking to the style of furniture from the Dutch Colonial Period, which was apparent in all the local productions. We immediately recognized the attraction, and felt that this would be a great way for us to create a much needed creative environment if and when the time was right. We didn't need a mansion to support our growth, and certainly not for my personal recovery, but simply a space that meant that we would be able to show our own style, both individually and collectively, and use this space to create cohesiveness. I had even planned the layout of my future home in my head, with the furniture arranged intelligently, and in such a way that it would enhance aspirations to heal and move on in life. Rose did remind me that I was prone to moving things around, and the proof was in the pudding as they say. She recalled how the interior of my living space would often spot various themes, and wondered where I actually had the energy to keep changing things around.

I must say that I inherited this trait from my mother and memories of "moving things around the house" never really evaded my mind. This was my time, the time to create a new atmosphere, in which, I would live with my illness, and make that an extension of my growth plan. I was all out to break the barriers, and noticed that to achieve this meant that I needed to demonstrate a special care for the things that I had selected, and for the living space that would inevitably house them. Both Rose and I had very strong inclinations towards creativity, and she had proven on many times, that she could be a major contributor to many of my ideas, even to the extent of turning a simple space into a mind stimulating area the moment we would encounter it. Needless to say, our purchases went overboard, but we were adamant to get this done. We made decisions with a purpose, and the remaining days on this amazing trip was a strong testament to being imaginative, taking chances, and exploring many interesting places in Lombok.

Lombok country side

Rose – Entrance to the temple grounds

Ancient Temple

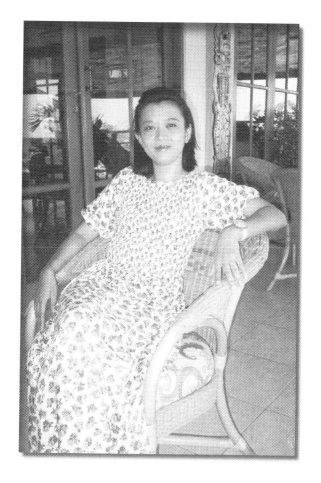

Rose in the breakfast Lounge

It was time for us to leave this remarkable island of Lombok and head home. The journey ahead was not going to be easy. I was suddenly reminded of the coming months, in which, I would need to endure intense chemotherapy after reversing the colostomy. I was excited and extremely apprehensive at the same time, but felt that the guiding voice in me would prevail, and continue to put me on the right path, show me the light during the anticipated days of gloom and doom, and pull me back to the path of light with immense possibilities. Before boarding the flight home, I looked back at all my travel notes and reminded myself that this was not going to be the last journey that I would take, and that if I was going to win this battle of living with my illness, I would need to make my mind run my body and never let the body tell the mind what to do. As we boarded the plane and settled into our seats, a quiet moment bestowed upon me, and gave me a quick glance of where life had taken me, and although I was up for a battle of mammoth proportions, I still had all my limbs and faculties to perform the necessary checks and balances, and this to me, was enough, I was ready to do battle.

Before we knew it, we touched down in Singapore at about 16.30pm local time.

14

The Power of Transformation

"However daunting the challenges we face, there's always a powerhouse of inspiration if we look deep within......."

Rose and I were happy to be home, although I was harbouring some feelings of dissatisfaction. I had just visited one of the most breathtakingly beautiful resorts in the world, and to come home to the concrete jungle of Singapore wasn't really that appetizing. Still, I had to face reality, and succumbed to the notion that there was now a mission at hand. I still remembered this day very clearly; it was February 14th, 1997, Valentines' Day. We stopped by the local store at the airport to buy some snacks, and I picked up the newspaper only to realize that old man Mr Asghar Hassan, my friend and mentor, had passed away. This was indeed a shock and it was only natural for me to abandon all plans for Valentines' Day, and made my way to the Hassan family home. Both Rose and I went home to unpack, and we braced ourselves to be with the family in Watten Estate, Singapore.

Upon reaching the family home, we noticed a huge crowd of people who had come to pay their respects. We sat down next to

Hamid and Suliman, as they were performing their prayers. Both of them had this empty and blank expression on their faces, which I found particularly difficult to grasp. After all, it was just a couple of months ago that Mr Hassan had visited me in the hospital, and kept me company in my darkest days, and now he was gone. It was surreal so to speak, and I spoke briefly to the family, extending my heartfelt condolences, and stayed for the next hour, talking to Hamid and his mother. As it was approaching the late evening, we said our farewells and made our way. As I was driving, I noticed Rose all quiet and I asked her if she was thinking about my imminent demise from this world, to which I was told to "shut up". That was the end of the conversation.

That evening, we sat down to a quiet Valentines' Day Dinner, and spoke about our holiday together, and starting planning our future as a married couple. I mentioned to Rose that based on what we choose to believe, we build up more and more answers to help us get through life. We acquire knowledge, full of facts, and the way things really are, we live through experiences, and we learn how life really is, we open up our imaginations, to the way that life could be, in our dreams, only to have arrived at this particular juncture. I said that no matter how we lived our lives, it was about the lives of people that we have touched and made a difference to. While we searched for answers and sometimes failed at that, we ended up searching for questions.

This was indeed about a transformation that we have entered into, and we reached that point together. Later that evening, I left Rose and went home to my little abode, my room which I was renting, and I said my prayers in silence before drifting off to a deep sleep. I woke up to a surprisingly glorious morning in Singapore and went about my day. I started by sorting out my camera and sent the films for developing. Yes, it was one of "those" cameras that functioned on film, but it took amazing photos, which I received after waiting patiently for a day or so. I couldn't wait to share the memories of the trip with my family in Malaysia, and after sorting out the rest of the day; I drove my Peugeot 405 back to Johor Bahru, and spent the rest of the week in my house in Bukit Kempas.

I had made it a point to jot down my thoughts during the trip and never realized that it would one day be used in a book. Let me share some of my thoughts here. In my early days of coming to terms with my illness, one of the greatest lessons that I had learnt was that feeling sorry for my-self was not the best way to deal with the uncertainties that were ahead of me. The way forward was to experience some form of enlightenment. While I wasn't really religious or practiced any form of meditation to experience enlightenment, I believed that this could truly be attained by being aware of the choices or options we have before us, no matter what the circumstances were. I was also taught very early in life that respecting others was key to my personal growth, and in this instance, respecting the point that others are entitled to making different choices, different believes, to arrive at different answers. Choosing to make decisions to move forward under circumstances, unforseen or otherwise, simply meant that I was able to create a much more conducive environment to live in. I wasn't really trying to make this world a better place, or to change its crumbling dynamics, I was merely searching for some truth in the present moment, and to understand what I was about to endure, which was an aggressive form of chemotherapy.

I had already researched the treatment modality, picked out my 'bandana', in case I went bald, and told myself that ultimately, the answers that I would carry with me will be the revelation of truth, and this was going to be my life's mission. However, little did I realize that in doing so, I attempted to persuade others that my life's choices were right while theirs were not! This resulted in an internal state of catastrophe, especially for me, and my immediate circle. I blamed everyone around me, I blamed them for stripping away all the mystery, the hype, and the success of leadership that I had written about before, and I blamed them for my 'nakedness'. In the end, I was left with nothing but silence, and I was left with no one but just myself. I felt incredibly isolated and alone, and I began to alienate myself from myself. I left that wonderful, living, breathing, unique and talented "me" in a world of complete isolation. I needed to come out of this quickly and looked for some transformation; this was a powerful state of affairs that I needed to restore. However, I was lost in transition; I was lost in reality and began to feel sorry for myself all over again. I hated this feeling.

Suddenly, the feeling of euphoria was gone, the thrill of having travelled to another dimension seemed no longer appealing, and depression began to set in. I was depressed for days, until it dawned on me that the only way out was to create some sense of drama in my life. I needed to look for a common denominator, and I finally found this in my work, my wonderful babies as I often referred to them, my Oriental Carpets. Believe it or not, but this was the beginning of my healing process. I could not wait to get back to work, but first I needed to get my affairs in order. The first step was to see Professor Abu Rauff to arrange for the reversal of my colostomy. I was dreaming about this freedom once again, to be able to appreciate my body without the presence of this alien object which was attached to it.

Not long after the end of the week, I scheduled an appointment with the good Professor and he gave me a remarkable and clean bill of health. Needless to say, the affected part of my colon had rested well over the past few months, and I was finally ready to undergo the surgery. The date was set, and I was once again wheeled into the operating theatre for the surgery. This time was different, as you can imagine. I was reinventing this sense of freedom, which up to this point seemed dim and unreachable. Prior to this, there appeared to be limited choices before me, and I was even made to believe that I needed to function on a rather remote level, with no adventure and basically surrendering to the illness. But I had a different view, and in my opinion, I had already promised myself that this life of mine needed to be an adventure, and I would do whatever I could, even if it meant breaking the rules.

I had nothing to lose now, and I did exactly that. I broke every rule in the book about surviving cancer, about living with cancer and in the end; I had more energy and perhaps the sheer audacity to look the illness in the face and tell it to go to hell. As human beings, I believed that we were already equipped with a sense of belonging that we needed to tap into, and this was more than a survival kit. This was a test of endurance to push myself to the end, and simply believe in the notion that my subconscious would always provide me with the answers. The choices were always available, perhaps not that clear in the beginning, due to undue fear and self-imposed stress, but it eventually revealed a clearer path, even to the extent of showing me the brutal side of reality. This was the powerful transformation that I needed to embrace, and I had to tell myself that either I believed I was going to get through the illness, or I would die. That was it, no negotiations and no bargaining. This was not only a matter of opinion, but a matter of belief and choice for the betterment of my well-being. So here I was, about to enter into this surgery that was inevitably one that would enable me to impress myself.

I woke up in the recovery room feeling very relieved that this was over. The first thing I did was to place my hands on the surgical site and there was no bag, I was free, finally free to be able to perform my bowel functions like a normal human being. Professor Abu Rauff informed my family and Rose who had already been camping outside the operating ward that everything went well. I was wheeled out and even though I was in pain, the sheer relief made me smile. I had a single room to myself, and it was the head-quarters for everyone to visit. This time my admission was at The National University – Singapore.

Later on in the evening, the attending nurse came in to my room to inform me that I needed to be on a drip, with no food or drink for at least a week. This would then be liberated with sips of water, before I would be allowed very small portions of clear soup which I absolutely detested, and finally on to normal food, but in very small doses. What I was longing for was to have the anal passage functioning again, to be able to control my bowels, and visit the toilet when I needed to normally. The day finally arrived, and to my great relief, the anastomosis which was performed by Professor Abu Rauff was successful – I had a glorious session in the bathroom. Who would have thought that a simple task of passing motion would be celebrated in such grand fashion? After ten days of hospitalization, it was time to return home to Malaysia.

This was early 1997 and my sister and Ruben had been planning their wedding. This was the first wedding in my immediate family, and needless to say, the buzz was in the air. The happy couple had also bought a lovely house in a cul-de-sac not far from the city centre in Johor Bahru, and before long, were planning to renovate their home, before moving in as a married couple. It was time for us to leave our modest home in Bukit Kempas, and while we were waiting for my recovery from surgery, the activities now centred on the grand wedding. My uncle Jegadeva in Kuala Lumpur very graciously offered his new home as the bride's house, and also agreed to give my sister away, considering that he was my father's brother, and now the eldest in the Kularatnam family clan. This was also the time that Rose was being introduced to the rest of my family and extended family - that would send a few tongues wagging, for obvious reasons, that I was soon going to convert and embrace Islam as my religion. While I still had time to look into this, the immediate task at hand was to introduce Rose to everyone, and the entire family took to her like a house on fire, well, that's how I felt anyway.

The wedding plans went into full throttle while I had another mission at hand — chemotherapy. This was the most dreaded part of healing which apparently was an absolute necessity. I was referred to Dr. Hwang Hwee Yong at Mt Elizabeth Hospital, who had pioneered a revolutionary method of administering the drug with very little physical side effects, but lethal nonetheless. After a few consultations, it was decided that I would need to have a port-a-catheter. In medicine, a port (or portacath) is a small medical appliance that is installed beneath the skin. A catheter connects the port to a vein. Under the skin, the port has a septum through which drugs can be injected and blood samples can be drawn many times, usually with less discomfort for the patient than a more typical "needle stick".

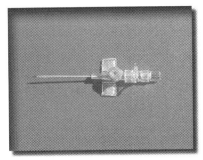

Images of the port with the needle assembly

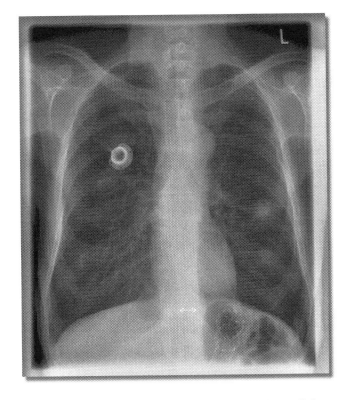

Image of a chest x-ray showing the positioning of the port

So there I was, back in the operating theatre to have this procedure done, and I have to say that this was not something that I was looking forward to. I had always told myself that although I was not an entirely brilliant or intelligent fellow like some of my fellow peers, I did, however, have a solid perception of reality, and this was my saving grace. It allowed me to take the dimensions of pain and fear onto another level of comprehension, much like an enigma in its own sense. Before long, I was out of the theatre and resting in the ward, when my surgeons came in to announce that everything went well. It was time to begin the chemotherapy and first thought was my hair, as I was petrified at the thought of looking like a cancer patient. To counter this minor issue, I had already purchased my preferred head gear and bandanna to create a new fashion statement.

During the course of chemotherapy which began almost immediately, I shuttled between my rented room in Singapore and the family home in Malaysia. Rose and I had purchased our very first car, a Peugeot 405 as I mentioned briefly before, and this was my mode of transportation. I also decided that I would return to work and endure this treatment while in the company of my wonderful rugs. The treatment began in the following days and I felt awful in the first few days. However, as I made my way back to work, I began to endure the treatment in a much better way. I used my work and my love for carpets as my primary tool for healing. I found that looking at carpets as a form of art became a story proponent towards benefiting my nervous system, while stimulating neurological brain signals. I found that appreciating carpets as an art form helped to relieve the aches and pains that I was enduring, almost on a daily basis. While I had the comfort of prescription drugs to create a sense of relief, this became a consistent regime that needed to be nurtured, and I was starting to form the habit of dependency on drugs all over again. I had to look at healing as an art form and this was a breakthrough, on all frontiers, because it allowed me to connect with my inner psyche, in which I had stored some of my creative juices, my creative appreciation premonitions.

In the course of the following months, I researched what artistic appreciation meant, and I found that through some form of expression and appreciation, I began to experience a change in attitude. I wasn't tensed or emotionally wired as I used to be, and I stopped blaming everyone around me for the state of trauma that I was in. I accepted responsibility for what was ahead of me, and this sincerely allowed me to release my body and imagination to a more permanent state of recognition. I was beginning to look at life more realistically and pragmatically, and ceased to operate on the notion that I needed to be a success. I was already a success, so there was no need to impress anyone. I just needed to function internally and impress myself, so to speak. While I was not a particularly artistic person, my appreciation for the art form encouraged the creative capacities to flow once again, and I was contributing this renewed and fresh perspective on my life at work in a much more prominent and positive way. I even mentioned to my superiors at work that they needed to look at me as if there was nothing wrong, and that I wasn't as fragile as they had made me out to be. This was definitely a contributing factor towards the curing process and before long; I was documenting over three hundred carpets and rugs for an all-important exhibition and sale in Malaysia. This was the powerhouse of inspiration that I was looking for.

The colour of life was another aspect that I had used in the process of healing. Since all the carpets and rugs that I had handled were filled with a kaleidoscope of colour and pattern, I looked at colour as a form of therapy. Colour therapy is a subject that has been researched widely, and within many cultures worldwide, and I found that colour therapy is a set of principles that can be used to create a harmonious and balanced setting for the purpose of healing, both internally and externally. According to the principles of this theory, colour reflects an energy state, and it is even a form of energy medicine, based on the belief that the human body is composed of energy fields, in which it can allow colour therapy to stimulate different parts of the brain. This certainly allowed me to work on the problems that I was facing in terms of energy deficiencies. I realized that this deficiency was the root cause of some of my physical and psychological responses that I had been displaying and experiencing thus far. While I was documenting and researching the literature on the rugs that were needed for the all-important exhibition, I came across a few pieces in this collection that certainly made an impression, and eventually stamped my love for this particular genre of rugs.

Carpets on display in one of my Exhibitions

**Signature Carpets and Collectibles From The
tents and cottages of Central Asia**

**Exhibition of Fine Persian and Oriental Carpets
and Modern Contemporary Rugs**

Showroom – A kaleidoscope of treasure

One of the unique features of this remarkable collection which I was privileged to have personally handled, and many more later on in my career, was the notion of colour, and I subconsciously began to select rugs with a particular set of tones. While researching this genre of antique village and city rugs, certain colours were defined and reflected as follows:-

Red: *Energy Stimulation*

Yellow: *Radiance and confidence*

Green: *Creativity and releases tension*

Blue: *Relaxation*

Violet: *Purity and simplicity of the mind*

As it turned out, my appreciation for the legacy in rug weaving collided in a way that it empowered my sense of purpose in life, and steered my journey towards recovery quite prominently. I found that this appreciation allowed me to express bold intentions, and gave me the tenacity and strength to pursue my mission at hand. This was simply to recover from my illness, and maintain a steady and firm grip on my footing towards establishing a better and much needed understanding of living with cancer. I must state that I do not profess to makes this a certainty, but the collision worked in a way that it helped me to reflect on the good times and, created mental images of joy from within. This, coupled with my sense of positive thinking, and being fully equipped with the much needed family support, enabled me to do battle with cancer.

**My remarkable support base – My mother,
sister, wife, brother in law and brother**

Living in the present moment was imperative, but realizing what I was able to achieve in the past before being diagnosed was a blueprint for me to persevere and move on, day by day, taking in and soaking up the twenty four hours that came with it.

During the course of the following months and before my sister's wedding, I travelled to Malaysia, Thailand, Indonesia and The Philippines for work, and in between my treatment, I found that I was willing to surrender to this appreciation for the art in carpets and rugs, knowing full well that if I were to succumb to the illness, I would go in comfort and this captured the very essence of living. This was a period of adjustment, and giving up was never going to be an option. Now I was able to enjoy the pleasantries and festivity of my sister's wedding...

The radiant couple – Priya and Ruben on their wedding day

15

Travelling through Triumph and Tragedy

"As fresh and new levels of anxiety pop up, it alters the orchestration of normal acceleration only to re-affirm the sense of purpose and belonging"

The wedding of the year was celebrated in full pomp and splendour with over one thousand guests, who had arrived from all over the country. Needless to say, my mother was the centre of attention, besides the bride and groom of course, and the endless entourage of family and friends. After the wedding, my sister and Ruben settled into their new home, while I went about my life at work, and started planning the next phase of travelling with Rose. She had purchased a "time share" plan that allowed members to travel all over the world, and stay in wonderful hotels for a specified period of time at no cost. This was a great way to save on accommodation, while touring interesting and fascinating places.

What was paramount to this next venture was the intensity of focus. I needed to balance my treatment with work, and the insatiable desire to explore the universe. I was also learning and reaching new levels at every important juncture, and at the time, it felt naturally difficult and challenging. Still, there was that desire to break the barriers of conformity or complacency, and after looking at our options, both Rose and I decided that we would travel to England and Spain. All through the years, I had come face to face with dilemma, and tested the virtues of courage in different situations. The first being surgery, when as much as it was needed, I often felt that I wished I had not agreed to all that undue pain and suffering. Fortunately, I prevailed, and stopped lamenting my own ego, while attesting to the fact that I had deserved the victory that was in the grasp of my hands. This was my personal victory against all the trials and tribulations over the last decade, and I wasn't going back to that dark corner again. It was time to roam the planet.

This was 1997, and the internet was fairly new, so we did not have much of an opportunity to research any of the places that we had planned to visit. The element of surprise and what we had gathered and seen in catalogues served as our only guide, coupled with the testimonies from a host of my cousins in 'The UK', and Rose's brother, Rohan, who was then studying in Loughborough University in Leicester. My eldest cousin Ahalia was living in London, and was only too pleased to offer her lovely house just off Portobello Road, so our accommodation was 'sorted'. After getting our affairs in order, we set out for The United Kingdom, and continued our journey on to Barcelona, Madrid and The Lovely Coastal Town of Salou. Rose and I boarded British Airways in late December 1997 and we were on our way. The journey to London's Heathrow was expected to take nine to ten hours I think, so it was going to be a real test for me personally. After surgery and chemotherapy, I had never imagined going on such a long drawn journey, but with the apparent excitement that was lingering in the air, and in between the in-flight movies on board the plane, I took to it like it was second nature. There was only one nagging problem, and that was overlooked at the time. I was constantly in need of the toilet - I had the feeling of losing control of my bowel functions, but thankfully it went well, and I managed to get through the journey. I didn't think too much of it then.

We landed as scheduled, and the first thing I did when we cleared customs was to ransack my bag to pull out my jacket and warm clothes. It was four degrees, and we were right in the middle of winter. Rose on the other hand, did not seem to mind the cold, and was getting by rather easily with just a layer of clothing and a pull over. I thought this was a great feat at first, but then I soon found out that her secret *"Jammu"* (Indonesian Herbal) pills were doing the trick. Anyway, my cousin and her husband Richard had braved the cold to meet us at the unearthly hour of six in the morning, and greeted us with huge hugs. It was so good to see them both, and after a short journey through the cold and grey winters' morning, we were sitting by the fire place in their lovely town house.

I must confess that deep down - I was rather pleased with myself, having made it half way across the world. I was aware that it was inevitably going to be a slight struggle, but it was the right choice then. The alternative option would always beckon, and does so adorned with fashionably good arguments. I've heard it all, it's not the right time, it's too risky, there will always be another time, what's the hurry, and the list goes on. Thankfully, I was blessed with great family support, and this spurred me on to make this trip. I often marvelled at some people who had that inner courage to step out and do things instinctively, while I had to put a great deal of thought into everything I did. My problem was the constant battle between courage and fear, while for others; it was about the consequence of being fearless. Well, I wanted to be fearless, after all, what did I have to lose? Being fearless may not end up in downfall, as some would attest to, but I was beginning to love that temperament, I adored its swagger and absence of manipulation. Being free and easy simply started to make a great deal of sense.

With my cousin Ahalia and her husband Richard

This was fundamentally the first trip to England and Europe, and both Rose and I were delightfully surprised at how well we adapted to the surroundings. The city of London was amazingly captivating, and we visited practically all the places of interest, either by car, where we would glance through the fogged up windscreen of my cousin's Peugeot 205, pointing towards the direction of Buckingham Palace, The Tower of London, Big Ben, to taking the rail (tram) and underground to The Victoria and Albert Museum, Portobello Road Market, or simply walking all over the city. It was an experience to say the least, but the best was yet to come. However, in between the excitement and euphoria of being in London, I began to experience intermittent bouts of bowel discomfort but attributed it to jet lag. I paid little attention to it, while I went about exploring the many delightful sights of this magical city.

The Victoria and Albert Museum

After spending a few days in London, we rented a car and drove to Warwick. Our accommodation was The Walton Hall Estate in Warwickshire. Historically, The Walton Hall was a 16th-century country mansion at Walton, near Welles Bourne, Warwickshire, once owned by Lord Field and the entertainer Danny La Rue.

Beyond the trivia, this was an absolutely beautiful estate to live in, and we were privy to this from the benefits that were accorded with Rose's 'time share' membership.

Walton estate – Late evening

In front of Walton Hall and by the fire place

You can probably imagine my feelings at this time. I remember when we first checked into this magnificent estate, we were ushered into our little manor, and right next to the living room window was the burial grounds of the ancestors. Shock horror! There was no way I was going to stay here, so we asked for a change of rooms, and we were taken to a private apartment wing on the fourth floor of a lovely restored building called the stables. In fact, it was previously an actual stable. This was a huge place, and we were informed of only one other family living on the floor below. To our utter disbelief, we heard the footsteps and voices of children coming from the upper floors running down the hallway. I'm not entirely sure about what transpired after this, but Rose reminded me that we wanted to speak to the manager the next morning after breakfast but forgot about it.

We knew that there was another unit occupied on the ground level and assumed that the kids were from there. We eventually mentioned this to the front desk staff when we were checking out who quietly told us that there was indeed another couple but they had no children. Oh My God!! What have we gotten ourselves into? Still, it was coming to the end of our journey so we thought little of it. To have arrived here after such a long journey was just too good to be true. Both Rose and I soaked up the amazing English country side and spent countless hours walking around the estate, -driving through the many smaller towns, where we would stop and have afternoon tea, complete with scones and muffins. It was like in the movies I tell you, just so exhilarating. I remember we only had a week in Warwick, and during this time, we visited the neighbouring districts like Shakespeare's birth-place where he lived with his wife, Anne Hathaway.

Shakespeare's Birth-Place

**Rose couldn't resist having her photo taken
in front of Ann Hathaway's Cottage**

Stow on the Wold – Cotswolds

Driving around the country side was such an effortless affair. We were equipped with just a road map and an instinctive sense of direction, and somehow everything fell into place. Thereafter we briefly drove through Bourton-On the Water, Moreton – In – Marsh and The Cotswolds

Lady Macbeth and Hamlet

The week was coming to an end and Rose wanted to visit her brother in Leicester, so after checking the map, we loaded up the Fiat Punto and started our journey. Before leaving, I made it a point to write a few things down about my experience with this triumphant journey. I had spent the last ten years living a life that was full of nothing but surprises. Despite the fact that

I had prevailed on all frontiers of a personal battle, and with the onset of illness, I was still learning, thinking, and trying to position myself on a platform of hammering out all the imminent issues that would eventually come my way. I would often spend countless hours and numerous days reflecting on issues until there was some clarity of thought. I wasn't really focusing on the details or specifics of any particular issue or problem, but on life in its entirety. Since the battle within to get over my illness needed a road map for recovery, I would conjure up the energy to setting the compass, getting my bearings right, and marshalling the arguments that I would be having with myself on what I should or should not do. However, I was now in a different mode so to speak. I wasn't really planning ahead, but just wanting to do as much as possible within the shortest possible time, because I was honestly and quietly operating under the notion that my time was up. The progressive moments needed to be aware of an individual time frame and its own success formula. In my case, success was on a day to day basis, and I would buy the next twenty four hours, and beyond that, was anyone's guess.

I suppose this journey and this trip was a means to reinventing my self-worth, while forging a bond with Rose. I wasn't about to be remembered as a hollow echo from once a formidable character, although reverberating still, but with little effect. I was going all out to live, love and love some more, in more ways possible, and this began with loving life to the fullest.

And so the next course of the trip began, and we visited Leicester, and spent the day with Rohan, Rose's brother. Leicester was an impressive city, and one that I was yearning to visit simply because my parents had studied in Leicester. It was memorable to be in Leicester, knowing that my folks had, at one time, dated and walked the same streets I was in.

Beyond this point, Rohan took over the driving and drove us around Leicester, and eventually all the way back to London, where we stayed with my cousin for a few more days. Being back in London was a great feeling, and we stayed up late, exchanging notes on our travels and even made it a point to do more shopping at the all too famous Portobello market, where I apparently had the audacity to bargain for an antique pirate's chest that I was interested in. This was not a done thing, or so I was told, but what the heck, I was in a market place, and it was only right to bargain. True to my ways, I managed to get a steal on this piece of old "junk" only to realize much later that it was indeed a piece of junk. Still, I had fun while it lasted. The journey in 'The UK' was drawing near, and Rohan left for Singapore, while Rose and I started to get ready for the next league of our journey – Barcelona and Spain.

Barcelona

We said our goodbyes and headed to London's Gatwick airport, which was then the airport in use because Heathrow had caught fire, so you can probably imagine the frenzy that was going on. We waited patiently, and it was our turn to fly out to Madrid, Spain. This was a brave move on my part – to take on another country in the thick of things, but I liked the boldness of the notion. I was venturing into a new dimension involving my personal relationship with Rose, and evidently, the country that we were about to visit. Rose's 'time share' membership rewarded us with a seven day stay at Sunning-dale village in Tenerife, on the Canary Islands.

We landed in Madrid and stayed the night before taking the next flight to Tenerife. That afternoon, we were greeted at the airport by ostentatious taxi drivers who were parading in all the latest European Cars, and the one that caught our attention was the Peugeot 406. I mean, come on, this was a luxury car back home, but not here. Needless to say, we jumped into the first one that drove up to us, and we made our way to our villa. Driving past the Spanish Coast was just awesome – the sea and the surrounding hills was a completely different scene from what we had experienced in London. This was an invariably grand setting, and I could not think of anything that would disturb or alter the mood of buoyancy. I knew then and there that I made the right decision, and I felt confident that both Rose and I would inevitably have the best seven days to come.

This was an amazing villa type accommodation which was perched precariously adjacent to the hills with the full ocean view to admire each and every day. What else could we have asked for?

Sunning Dale Village on the Canary Island, Tenerife

If I were to describe Spain in one phrase, it would be "quintessentially decent". Everything seemed to be in perfect harmony. There was no traffic besides what was apparent in the main city streets, no one was rushing about, and the seemingly apparent mood of tranquil was prevalent everywhere we looked. I was in a genuine quandary as to whether I should just stay here. We arrived at Sunning-dale and settled in quickly before heading out to explore the sights and quiet night life.

House of Balconies – La Oratava - Tenerife

Food was available in abundance, and Rose was quickly taken in with the spread of seafood in all the restaurants that we visited. She still talks about this to this day! Perhaps one day we might just decide to re- visit this amazing country. The following days went by in a relatively quiet, yet exhilarating fashion. It was during this memorable week that Rose taught me to recite the 'Al- Fatiha'.

In Islam, "**Sūrat al-Fātiḥah**" (Arabic: سورة الفاتحـــة), is the first chapter of the Quran. Its seven "*ayat*" (verses) are a prayer for God's guidance, and stresses His Lordship and Mercy. This chapter has an essential role in "*Salaat*" (daily prayer); and Muslims should recite the "sura Al-Fatiha" seventeen times a day in "*Fard*" (compulsory) "Salaat", at the start of each unit of prayer. It took me a day to master this verse".

One of the highlights of the Canary Islands was a visit to Mount Tiede, with a peak of 3,718 m, the highest peak of Spain. This mountain was also known as the sleeping volcano, the third largest in the world, which was last active in 1909.

The peak was practically all year under the snow, and it's a trademark of the island, so it's no surprise that Tenerife means "white mountain". We planned a bus trip to the peak which at the time was a dormant volcanic crater. Rose and I actually stood right in the middle of this crater despite the freezing cold. You're not going to believe this but shortly after our visit, and this was perhaps when we returned to Singapore, that we heard that Mount Tiede actually erupted. So there you have it, how uncanny, that we were probably one of the few people who actually got to admire the sheer beauty of this white peak before it erupted!

Freezing Cold – Mt Tiede – Volcanic Crater

From then on, I remember the days when we would venture out into the coastal town of Salou by bus and train, not knowing where we would end up, only to be greeted by this awesome sight…

Hanging out in Salou

Next on our list was to head back to Madrid and Barcelona, and tour a few more places of interest, before heading back to London. The city skyline was just too good to be true, and the frenzy along Avinguda Diagonal in Barcelona's La Ramblas was an eye opener.

Amazing street entertainers – La Ramblas

I reflected on the awesome nature of this beautiful country, of the weight on my shoulders, the pain and excitement, as this was the time when I was really starting to feel immense pressure in my intestinal tract. I asked myself, "How much more can I endure, especially when I was so far away from home". Still, the thought of dying did cross my mind, but I wasn't about to get my head chopped off if I had mentioned this to Rose. I kept telling myself that I was fine, and perhaps the discomfort that I was feeling was all due to indigestion, too much eating, and of the good life. It was time to tough it out. The journey was still incomplete, as we needed to head back to the city and check into one of the local hotels before flying out to London.

This was late December, 1997 and I remember the news on the television about a Singapore Airlines crash. This was a horrifying incident and both Rose and I were in shock. True to my incorrigible ways, I decided to surf the free porn channels on the European Television network instead. Yes, I know what a thing to do at a time like this! But let me elaborate more articulately on what I was trying to achieve, and you can ignore the porn channels for a while! In this time, I was trying to wear what I would aptly describe as psychological armour, a protective gear which would prevent any arrows from attacking me. I felt that the pain was becoming quite unbearable, was much like a piercing dagger through my belly. I needed to achieve some kind of weightlessness which would allow my body to float. Am I making any sense I thought! I wasn't about to give in to any pain at this juncture, there was free porn on the TV remember?

Rose was speechless, and pretended to do her thing while I had this perpetual grin on my face. Despite the imminent discomfort, I felt enormously confident of what I was doing. The reason for this was I felt that I was on top of things, and I had the energy to travel, and as early as possible after surgery and chemotherapy. While each step was a struggle, I was ready to do battle, to get up each day and face the challenges ahead, and fight whatever might be barring the path, often with a certain degree of anxiety - with a combination of some fear and being reckless about my own destiny. I was adamant that I needed to break the barriers that were in front of me and stop entertaining the pain. Although I had made some odd compromises along the way, but by and large, and for the first time since my ordeal with cancer, I felt that I was guided by what I genuinely thought was the right choice for me to prevail. As my brother Rajiv mentioned in his introduction, "If misdirected emotions or ideas can be transformed into illness, why could not illness disappear through a transformation into an idea"?

The following morning, we packed up after breakfast, and after a short walk around the city of Madrid; we headed to the airport, for the onward trip to London. We had a couple of days in London, and my cousin played host again. We visited a few Irish pubs and did some shopping. I remember visiting Harrods of London, opulent to say the least.

It was time to leave London and head home. We said our goodbyes to my cousin and took the train to the airport. Later in the night before boarding British Airways for Singapore, I had my very first scare with pain. It was excruciating, but I decided to keep this to myself. This was when it became apparent that there would be no clear departure from all this discomfort unless I sought medical help. Both Rose and I settled into our seats and flew home. We landed in Changi Airport Singapore, and Rohan was there to pick us up in our car, this time we had traded in the Peugeot for a Mazda 626, a sportier two litre engine that took off like a rocket. Rose loved it, and judging by the way Rohan was 'clipping' the corners of the road, I could tell that he loved it too. We made our way home and by then, I was already staying in a rented apartment in Singapore after having moved out of Bukit Kempas in Johor Bahru, Malaysia. I had also given up the rented room that I was in for a while, and I had a nice little two bedroom apartment in Toa Payoh's busy HDB (Housing Development Board) vicinity. I simply adored this neighbourhood and it was even more convenient since Rose was staying just a stones' throw in the next street with her mother and family. We made our respective ways to settle into our respective homes and caught up later than evening for dinner. All the Indonesian teak furniture that we had purchased on our earlier trip to Lombok was still in one piece in my apartment, and I was pleased to be home. Later that night, before retiring to bed, I had a very strong premonition that I was about to face cancer again, but I had no inclination of its magnitude and force. Sleep deprived, it was just a matter of minutes before I was in deep sleep.

Waking up to the morning's sunshine was a breather of relief, especially since I had just spent the last month in the cold. While I was missing the suiting up in jackets and long coats, it was nice to be in the warmth of Singapore's weather. I unpacked and called up the office to mention that I was back from the trip. I always felt that the natural progression of things had to create a different set of paradigms about survival, and this was also needed in my quest to gather the much needed support and understanding from the people in my immediate circle. This deeper spread of support was now slowly but surely dwindling, as I began to gauge that the folks at work were becoming less accommodating or understanding about my mission in life. Perhaps my departure from the work scene for an extended period of time may have taken its toll on the level of patience that I had once received unconditionally, and perhaps taken for granted. To some, this might seem like the correlation of two completely separate issues, but to me, it indicated a significant shift, particularly in social attitudes. Would it have been asking for too much if all I wanted was some space to heal? Even if this meant that I would require some time off work? Well, apparently not. I suppose the remarks that were passed at work defined a different paradigm and the same group of people who, not long ago, had wanted to finish me off with their voodoo nonsense, was back at play.

I even heard comments like, "what you do with your personal life is your problem but what you do to others is not"! Go figure! I could not understand this sudden departure from normal propriety, and after some prodding and relentless phone calls, it was revealed to me that some folks in the company were insanely jealous of the fact that the management was still paying my salary and commissions, despite the fact that I had been absent from work over a considerable period of time. So there you have it, the plot thickens! I couldn't care less about this somewhat real-life drama and idiotic conundrum. I went about my days and nights, and when the time was right, I returned to work. Although I had the management on my side, I still had to make a point and made it known that I was not going to be threatened by their nonsense again, not the second time around. There would be no unwanted visitors coming into my life anymore, for I had already left that part of my life in another dimension a long time ago. True to my ways and my disposition on life's challenges, I took on my work and responsibilities head on. Although I thought that the way the issues were played out revealed something of the changing nature of professional relationships, I wasn't entirely surprised at the level of immaturity that was clear before me.

So now, on top of my illness, I had to watch my back, and ensure that I wasn't going to be stabbed when I least expected it. I had travelled through a triumphant stage and dealt with some minor bouts of tragedy along the way, so now, it was time to push ahead, and find that edge, that would re-affirm my sense of purpose and belonging. I certainly belonged to the space that I was in - I had made a difference, and I was not in any mood to let anyone take that away from me. I had complete clarity about what it was I had to do, and I really did feel the height of my ability. I felt that despite my recent bout with surgery and treatment, I was still on top of my game. On some remote level, I appreciated the bitter irony that this had happened on my own turf, and even though my popularity was now being altered, it was more of my ego being bashed, and so I told myself that this needed to stop. I wrote about my sense of being a leader of the pack, and I continued to recognize the fact that there was a residual respect between myself and the top management of the company, and I persevered to protect that.

In the following days, I shared the photos that I had taken from the Victoria and Albert Museum in London and showed the bosses a picture of one of the oldest carpet that was known in existence, prior to the discovery of the Pazyryk Carpet (the oldest carpet in the world). I was fortunate to have viewed the Ardebil Carpet in its entirety. This was a treasure trove, one that every carpet dealer must see, at least once in their lifetime.

16

Postscript

"Opulence redefined"

The year was 1998, and it looked like it was going to involve actions that would inevitably test the boundaries of sanity. My professional life had survived after a minor setback in the early months of 1998, so I took it upon myself to indulge deeper into the art of carpet appreciation. I began appearing on Singapore's Asian business news, and was interviewed on various aspects of collecting and appreciating carpets as an investment. Eventually, it was just a matter of time, that there was some discussion about an eventual rise to the top management level. I wasn't aware of this immediately, until a mutual friend, our banker, revealed that the two bosses were planning to include me in the line up to take over the company. I was just thirty four years old, and I thought that this would have had monumental consequences if the news were to spread amongst the rest of the crew. Still, I was absolutely thrilled at the prospects, but I thought to myself that I should let things set its course.

I had also mentioned to Rose about the behaviour of the motley crew back in the office, and while Rose was known not to comment without reason, that would not mean that she would remain quiet, and she would let you have a solid 'ear bashing' if that's what it took to wake you up! While she also felt that I should talk less and do more, it was now a matter of whether I should say something to the management, or let "sleeping dogs lie" - there was no need to instigate trouble and test fate. So that was it, and the rest was pretty much ordained in destiny. As it was approaching the middle of the year, both Rose and I decided that we would start apartment hunting, in case we stumbled upon a great deal. Not long after the search, we found a beautiful two storey apartment and went ahead with the purchase. However, as fate would have it, I had another bout with cancer and this time, it was back with a vengeance. After meeting with my team of doctors, it was revealed to me that the colostomy needed to be re-attached; apparently all the bouts of discomfort that I had experienced when I was travelling in December 1997 were clear symptoms of a recurrent tumour.

So it was decided without much deliberation, that due to the intensity of the recurrence, the surgery needed to be done immediately. Besides the aggressive tumour in the large intestines, there were other issues in my spinal cord, pelvic region, and bladder, so it was decided that a partial pelvic exenteration would be the preferred cause of action. According to the journal of medicine, pelvic exenteration is the most extensive pelvic surgery. It's used most often when cancer has recurred and involves removing a small part or the entire bladder, part of the lower bowel, (rectum) and the prostate. This operation is only done if there are no signs of cancer anywhere else in the body, so my doctors assured me that even though this radical surgery was expected to take eight to ten hours, the recovery would be prolonged, but certainly possible. There was some hope I must say. Dr Hwang, my Oncologist from Mt Elizabeth, was summoned to the ward, and made it a point to inform my family that she would do everything to help, and to ensure that the best treatment be made possible. I asked the doctors about the surgery that was done in 1996, and if the reversal of the temporary colostomy had anything to do with this sudden turn of events. From what I gathered, if anyone had been diagnosed with stage four rectum cancer in the West, there was only one choice available, and that involved removing the entire colon and rectum, and the colostomy would need to be permanent. At this time, I could only think of enduring the next few days in very small baby steps, as I was not able to comprehend the magnitude and scale of this surgery. My family was just incredible, and Rose was at my bedside every day, right from the beginning of this ordeal, despite her busy schedule from running her renovation business and juggling the household affairs. The surgery went according to plan, and while I was about to go under anaesthesia for the umpteen time, I couldn't help but think of the huge strain this must have been on my immediate family. I'm sure there was a cloud of uncertainty and insecurity hanging over them, while they waited for the surgery to be over. For some strange and unexplained reason, I wasn't afraid, not like before, and I went under the knife knowing full well that everything would work out well.

Waking up in the recovery ward in the operating theatre, I sensed some relief, but was nonetheless in indescribable pain. Needless to say, I was craving for pain relief and the pethidine injections, coupled with Morphine doses were already being administered, not together but in some combination alternatively. I was wheeled into the ward in Mt. Elizabeth Hospital – a four bedded room with a view of the city from the side window. My family was already waiting, and I was very relieved to see everyone there. I must profess to the fact that family, though intimately involved in the lives of their loved ones, is somewhat detached from the real situation. Even though they witness the events and are privy to the moments of joy and pain, I couldn't help but feel that they felt like bystanders, because inevitably, in the end, they are just that. They stand by you and watch you get in and out of consciousness, but are unable to do anything for you. This must have been incredibly frustrating for my family, especially my mother, who had to watch her eldest son face so much pain, and perhaps even death. Prior to this ordeal, I would often attest to the fact that while family are sometimes relieved of the intense pain and pressure that is the patient's alone, they are never relieved of the scrutiny. And to make matters worse, they could see what I was going through, but let's face it, I would often give them the impression that everything was fine, and that gave them a feeling of being even more alienated. They may have appeared to be an integral part of my ordeal but were nonetheless never wholly involved. I don't know what I would have done if I was on the other side of the bed watching my mother, brother or sister in pain. That would have been incredibly difficult.

Professor Abu Rauff was seen in and out of the ward and my room. I remember one particular morning, when he came in to deliver some very bad and disturbing news. Apparently, the results from the tissue samples that were taken from my intestines during surgery, revealed that my conditioned had worsened, and I was now looking at very limited time left to live, although this was not revealed to me at the time. I did notice my doctors and even Dr Hwang in tears when they came to visit me, and Professor Rauff further reiterated that he had mentioned to us all prior to the surgery, that I was perhaps facing a life altering surgery and prognosis - which only meant one thing, that the cancer was spreading. We, of course, were oblivious to this.

This was day three, post-operative, and on one afternoon, who do I see walking into the ward, but my brother Rajiv, who was apparently informed of my condition while he was in Adelaide. Rajiv was working for an Australian firm then, and was about five or six years into his professional practice as an Architect. I was so surprised to see him, and while I was able to talk and comprehend everything around me, I took advantage of the situation and engaged in countless hours of family bonding. I even remember Rajiv insisting that I needed a shave and went on to do just that, leaving me with a Charles Bronson moustache! I couldn't help but feel how real I was with my family around me. At times, I could be most angry, most loving, and even most suffocated, but more often, most motivated. I know that being a cancer patient did not give me the right to be selfish, but I was, at times, and when I would think of how horrible it made me feel, and what it was possibly doing to my family, the feeling of belonging to a family unit drags you back to your need for, and your commitment to, your family, and the company of people in your inner circle. While writing this note, I looked up some writings on family dynamics, and The Honourable Tony Blair, Former Prime Minister of Britain sums it up brilliantly. In his memoirs, he writes:-

> *"In the family, there are a few hidden spaces, few facets of character, good or bad, that lie undiscovered, few delusions and even fewer fantasies. There are many glimpses of the best and the worst of the human being. In the end, most important of all, you have to forgive the trespasses in order that yours too can be forgiven. And just occasionally, you espy the essential strength that the family represents, and realize it is a marvel of human achievement and for all its shortcomings, anxieties and tensions, greatly to be cherished".*

Simply put, I wouldn't be here today if not for my family. My mother, who took a very long time to regain her independence after my father's death, understandably needed the time and space to get her life back. Her children gave her the time she needed, but she also needed that added nudge to get out and do things on her own. To this, I must thank my sister, who has been tremendously instrumental in pushing my mother onto a platform of independence and freedom. All throughout these years, my mother has been a rock to me, a great pillar of strength. She remained strong when I was weak, even more determined when I began to show signs of faltering, and remained very protective of her children and the family dynamics, and to this day, I will never forget this remarkable woman, despite all our frequent bouts of disagreements, and stood by me despite all the odds. When you come from a family like mine, there comes a time when people want to know everything, and this can be bloody annoying. And when the attack seems to be vehemently relentless, that's when all hell breaks loose. So now, we have adopted a different approach to family dynamics, we allow each other the space to grow and roam freely, with no judgements, no comments made, and just to bask in the glory of mutual adoration and pure love. Not too much to ask for is it?

After what felt like an eternity, I was told that there was nothing more that the doctors could do and it was time to return home, although I had no idea that this meant "go home and get your affairs in order". My sister and Ruben very graciously took me into their new home in Bandar Baru Uda, a trendy and new residential area where only the top brass lived. You can see that my sister and Ruben were rolling with the high society. I had a room to myself, and with my mother being with me, the next couple of months went by with nothing short of "drama".

At this point, I had developed a very strong need for pain killers, and this was 'bumped up a notch' with the inclusion of intravenous injections of pain medications, that practically slowed down my heart rate and put me into a very deep sleep. There was a doctor in Johor Bahru who ran a private practice, and she was one day called in to attend to a distressed patient, only to find out that there was a distressed parent too - my mother.

This Doctor started to administer some very potent combinations of injections that enabled me to go into a sleep like state, almost unperturbed of my surroundings, and I began to enjoy this sense of euphoria. Eventually, the Doctor moved into the house and began to administer the injections every four hours. My sister and Ruben were very patient until one final day, when Ruben stepped up and told me that if I wanted to kill myself, then I should do so in my own home. This was a huge wake up call, for I had apparently been given a lethal dose that morning and my heart almost stopped. The Doctor and my mother were sitting by my bedside in a silent prayer because they honestly thought that my time was up. Thankfully, Ruben came to his senses and was adamant in getting rid of this Doctor, and I was left to succumb to the pressures and signs of severe withdrawal symptoms. This was also the time that Ruben mentioned that I had been given three weeks to live, and that the family was planning my funeral. This explains why my brother was summoned earlier.

People deal with pressure in all kinds of different ways, especially terminally ill patients. Naturally, my altered state of consciousness was no help to my recovery, and I needed to be placed on a strict regime of round the clock monitoring. My aunts from all the country began to visit on a more regular basis, and I was made to believe that surviving this ordeal was indeed a possibility; an eventual and positive outcome was clearly visible. I had no means to deal with this other than to take each day as it came. The pressure was just too great, and this tested the proclamation of my very existence. I always admired myself as a person with extraordinary character, strong and resolute, and often willing to endure as much as possible to strive ahead, despite the muddled human affairs. Then I realized that I did not exist along the parameters of this revelation simply because I knew that I needed help. I knew that I wasn't able to be selfless, and to put my life on the line to proof that I was this person of character. This was absurd. Life to me was always a gift from God, and I needed to live this life to the fullest, and with some sense of purpose – nothing more.

But privilege though it is, I became aware over time, of the consequences of each good or bad decision. I began to realize that the destructive behaviour of mine needed to cease. While fear and personal insecurity came across as terrible factors in my daily life, I needed to reduce this to dramatically improve my state of being. Over time and in the following months, I began to regain my strength, and was slowly reducing my medication intake. I was able to ambulate freely, and it was at this time that I decided to return to work. I was on a permanent colostomy, and this would have been the very first time that I was attempting to be in a social and professional setting with the colostomy. It was terrifying to say the least, and I can remember the numerous embarrassing moments I had when the stoma bag would leak, emitting a foul odour in the air. Thankfully, I was never in a compromising situation that required the people around me to run for their lives. This was soon resonating well with my sense of wellbeing, and I could see myself recovering, despite the prognosis from the

Doctors in Singapore that I had very limited time left. After all, this was now almost six months after surgery, and way past my three week deadline! It was time to summon some draconian powers within me. This was also the time when I realized that people around me, undesirable elements perhaps, began to talk and I began to recognize things that were carried on the voice. I realized that words and behaviour began to spell something to me, and what became obvious were all the subtleties, and this was a constant reminder of how certain dynamics that I would take for granted, could easily change.

In the following months throughout my recovery, I started a different regime – not the one that I used to employ, which involved a regime of drugs and retiring to the notion of being "high", but one that involved making more sense of what was transpiring, and to deal with the intermittent bouts of mind altering bombardments. Now, I was exposing myself to a different kind of stimuli, one that was more embedded in my mind, and one that appeared to be more natural. The first was to move my life into a more permanent environment, and this meant moving back to Singapore, and this was when Rose and I decided that we would tie the knot. I never really had the opportunity to get down on my knees and propose to Rose in a romantic fashion, and to this day, I regret not having done so. This remarkable woman agreed to marry me under such difficult and testing circumstances, and we began to look at the possibility of purchasing our very first home together as a married couple. But first, I needed to attend to converting to Islam, and I registered for the conversion classes. I learnt a great deal about the religion, and what it meant to live my life in this new environment that I was about to enter. I was still under the influence of drugs, but this was a more controlled regime of doses, strictly monitored, and this was a choice that I needed to make. I did not have the luxury of 'screwing up my life' and dragging everyone down with me.

I remembered the days of being in hospital in a solitary confinement like setting, staring at the ceiling and watching the clock tick, anxiously waiting for my next injection of pethidine. Ironically, this watchful way extended the element of humanity and human nature by itself. Nonverbal actions, language and words, positive factors, actions and consequences, enabled me to reach deep within. I examined the very core of my existence, and wondered about the family history of cancer, and how I had re-visited this twice, and could not ignore the fact that cancer had claimed the lives of almost all the first born males on my paternal side between the ages of thirty five to fifty. During the years in hospital, I looked at everyone's body language, and I was able to tell if my care givers were going to deliver good or bad news. I learned to read their faces, and I learned to read my medical charts, and while some of the data made no sense, it used to amuse me to the point of being able to understand my own reactions to any particular situation or situations. I suppose, I was able to roam in my mind freely, and was capable of a certain level of intelligence nurtured by the quietness and internal attachments.

Armed with a renewed sense of achievement and with all my batteries re-charged, Rose and I began to look at HDB houses, and after what was an exhausting period of having looked at more than twenty apartments all over the island, we finally settled on a HDB apartment, not too far from her mother's apartment in Toa Payoh. As luck would have it, apparently we had seen this very same apartment about a year ago, when it was priced at its peak. I also recall that prior to my moving into my sister's house in Johor Bahru in 1998, Rose and I lost our two storey apartment which we had purchased earlier, due to the prevailing circumstances at the time. Perhaps this was serendipity playing out all over again, and it was as sweet as ever, since we managed to secure the apartment for a whole lot less than what we would have paid a year before. Everything happens for a reason, or so I'm told, and I'm not about to argue with this notion of truth. For the next couple of months before getting married, I attended the religious and conversion classes while attending to my duties at work in full fashion. I was back in the game, and I was slowly but surely recovering. On one glorious morning, I recited the "Kalimah Shahadah" (declaration of faith) which is in two parts, the unity and oneness of "Allah" and the acceptance of Prophet Hood. After successfully reciting the verse, I converted to Islam and took the name Mohammad Adam Kuladeva, although I have retained my birth name to this day. Rose and I were officially married on the 15th of October 1998, in the company of our close family members and friends. This was just six years after my very first diagnosis with cancer and almost ten years since the day we met.

Wedding day

I often wondered about where I would have ended up if I hadn't stumbled upon the carpet shop (boutique) in Melbourne back in my student days, and talked incessantly about the carpet that I fell in love with. This was the moment that eventually enabled me to travel to Singapore. My brother Rajiv talks about my attempt to gather instead of collect, and that thoughts and processes are somewhat internal, drawing from the point of illness, and how I arrived at that particular point in my life when the love for the arts and its magnificent healing properties began to surface. Rightfully, this discourse may be questionable to some, but the marriage of ideals has worked well for me, and in the quest to prevail, I have embarked on an audacious mission to reach out to as many people as possible, while trying to establish the equilibrium surrounding my existence, to create and hopefully maintain, a rich experience which is nothing short of rewarding and euphoric. Some concepts are beyond the reach of words because they concern the innermost self, and have much more to do with emotions. This journey is only the beginning to what I hope will be an endless affair of love, life, and precious friendships. As I see the world the way it is, and within me, the connections that have been made and rekindled, have set forth a renewed level of energy and spirit, and I will pursue the course to protect and frame its disposition abundantly with full vigour and a force to be reckoned with. Giving up was never an option, but living this life with extraordinary audacity has certainly been justifiable. It has transcended, transformed and catapulted my spirits to a whole new level, bordering on redefining opulence and grace.

The Great Wall of China

The experience begins.......

About the Author

Dhush Kuladeva is the Founder and CEO of The Gallery-Exclusive and is a seasoned practitioner with over 25 years in the field of luxury retailing, specializing in the area of Supreme and Exquisite Oriental Carpets. He is currently heading business expansions in Vietnam, Cambodia, Singapore, and Malaysia, and has taken the business into the commercial, residential and hospitality segments respectively. Over the years, Dhush has served various industries including management services, advertising, total integrated design consultancy, business coaching, corporate communications, and public relations. He graduated with a degree in Social Sciences from Deakin Warrnambool University in Australia.

He is married to his life-long companion Rozana, and has a home in Singapore, and shuttles frequently between his family home and Vietnam.

Printed in the United States
By Bookmasters